KAY'S MARVELLOUS MEDICINE

KAY'S MARVELLOUS MEDICINE

A GROSS AND GRUESOME HISTORY OF THE HUMAN BODY

ADAM KAY

ILLUSTRATED BY HENRY PAKER

PUFFIN

PUFFIN BOOKS

UK | USA | Canada | Ireland | Australia
India | New Zealand | South Africa

Puffin Books is part of the Penguin Random House group of companies
whose addresses can be found at global.penguinrandomhouse.com

www.penguin.co.uk   www.puffin.co.uk   www.ladybird.co.uk

First published 2021

001

With thanks to Inclusive Minds

TOBLERONE is a trade mark belonging to Kraft Foods, Schweiz Holding GmbH

Text design by Perfect Bound Ltd
Printed in Great Britain by Clays Ltd, Elcograf S.p.A.

The authorized representative in the EEA is Penguin Random House Ireland,
Morrison Chambers, 32 Nassau Street, Dublin D02 YH68

A CIP catalogue record for this book is available from the British Library

HARDBACK
ISBN: 978–0–241–50852–7

INTERNATIONAL PAPERBACK
ISBN: 978–0–241–50853–4

All correspondence to:
Puffin Books, Penguin Random House Children's
One Embassy Gardens, 8 Viaduct Gardens, London SW11 7BW

To Michael Sharpington, who did an amazing fart at school,

which lasted over a minute, and was known forever

afterwards as Michael Fartington.

And with thanks to my Great Aunt Prunella

for reading an early draft of this book

and giving me her thoughts.

CONTENTS

MAJOR MEDICAL

1600 BC (ANCIENT EGYPT)

Doctors discovered that the heart pumps blood around the body. But then again, they also reckoned that poo flowed out of the heart . . .

400 BC (ANCIENT GREECE)

Hippocrates realized that illnesses aren't caused by magic. Apologies if you thought that illnesses were caused by magic and this is a massive spoiler.

1928

Antibiotics were discovered by Sir Alexander Antibiotic. I mean Sir Antibiotic Fleming. Sorry, Sir Alexander Fleming. That's better.

1910

Marie Curie discovered radiation and then everyone's houses were nice and warm. No, hang on, that's radiators. Radiation is a treatment for cancer.

1929

Doctors discovered that smoking was dangerous. Before then, doctors thought smoking was good for you – I don't like to call people idiots, but . . .

1954

The first kidney transplant took place, soon followed by liver transplants, heart transplants and bum transplants. (Maybe not bum transplants, actually.)

MOMENTS

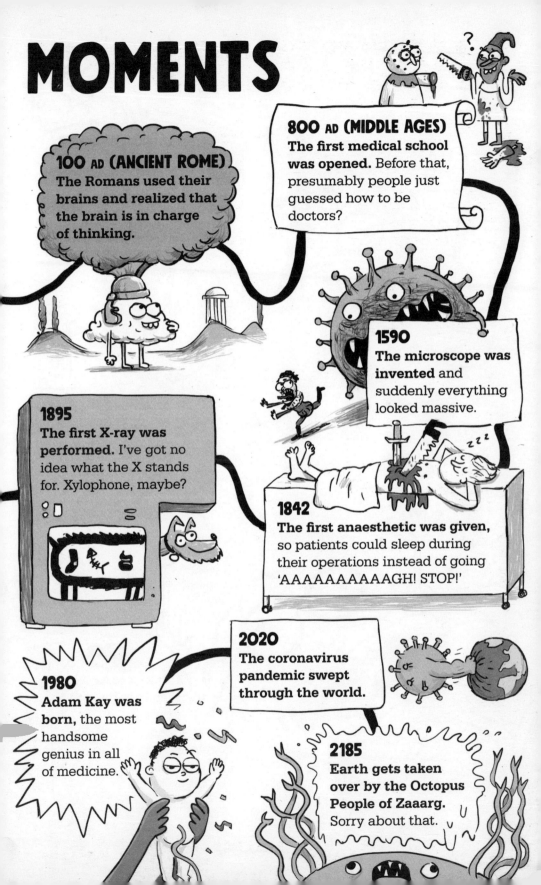

100 AD (ANCIENT ROME)
The Romans used their brains and realized that the brain is in charge of thinking.

800 AD (MIDDLE AGES)
The first medical school was opened. Before that, presumably people just guessed how to be doctors?

1590
The microscope was invented and suddenly everything looked massive.

1895
The first X-ray was performed. I've got no idea what the X stands for. Xylophone, maybe?

1842
The first anaesthetic was given, so patients could sleep during their operations instead of going 'AAAAAAAAAAGH! STOP!'

2020
The coronavirus pandemic swept through the world.

1980
Adam Kay was born, the most handsome genius in all of medicine.

2185
Earth gets taken over by the Octopus People of Zaaarg. Sorry about that.

THE BIT AT THE START

WHERE YOU FIND OUT WHAT THE BOOK IS ABOUT

(also known as INTRODUCTION)

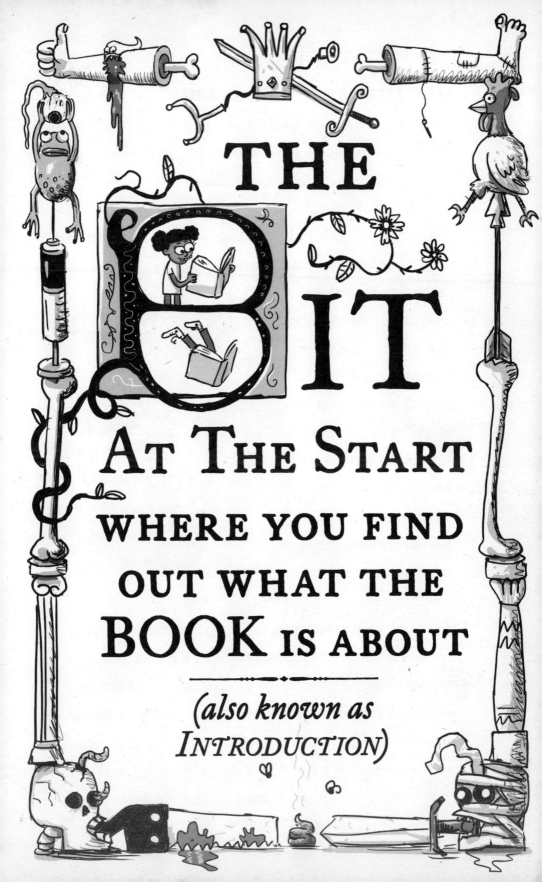

LET'S TALK ABOUT THE OLDEN DAYS. No, not last Christmas – we need to go even further back than that. Where are you now? Dinosaurs. Nope, you've gone too far. Forward a bit – right, that's better.

When you think about history, you might imagine knights in clunky-looking armour riding off into battle, or Ancient Egyptians building pyramids, or kings and queens chopping people's heads off. You might have heard of poo plopping its way down the streets because no one had invented toilets yet, and grown-ups forcing children to climb up chimneys.

Quite right too – might as well make lazy, stinking children do some work for once in their miserable lives. Prunella

While all this was going on, one thing stayed pretty much the same: the human body. The doctor you saw last week about those spots on your bum (don't worry, I won't tell anyone) was just the latest in a long line of doctors who've been examining people's bums – and various other body parts – for centuries. But I'm pretty sure that the doctor you saw was a bit different from the

6

ones in Ancient Egypt. First of all, she probably had better teeth and didn't wear a massive gold headdress. (I wish I'd been allowed to wear a massive gold headdress when I was a doctor.) More importantly, she knows an awful lot more about the human body than people did back then.

That was the main problem with the olden days – people didn't have the slightest clue how our bodies worked. So if you got ill, even if it was something really minor, like bum-spots, you could be in massive trouble. And the cure for your unfortunate bum-spots (how are they doing now, by the way?) would've been something mega-weird and useless – like gargling with wee or shoving insects down your pants.

I HAVE REMOVED YOUR BUM-SPOTS. AND YOUR BUM.

Don't believe me? Well, how do you and your spotty bum fancy a bit of time travel? It's OK – you don't need a packed lunch, and there's no chance of changing history by accidentally sneezing on Julius Caesar and somehow causing the human race to be overthrown by earthworms.

We'll head back thousands of years to see how doctors of the past muddled through without all those things that now save our lives every single day, from anaesthetics and antibiotics all the way to X-rays and . . . umm . . . something else beginning with X. Plus, we'll look at all the mistakes and experiments (mostly mistakes, to be honest) that eventually led to us figuring out how everything works. When I say 'us', I mean famous scientists of the past – **YOU** didn't discover how any of the body works. ——→ *Nor did you, Adam, you useless weasel. Prunella*

I'll answer all the questions you didn't even realize you had to ask, like:

WHAT HAPPENED IF YOU NEEDED A TOP-UP OF BLOOD BEFORE BLOOD TRANSFUSIONS WERE INVENTED?

It depends on which doctor you saw, but they might have told you to drink wee, or beer, or even dog's blood. I don't want to spoil the surprise, but none of those treatments worked particularly well . . .

WHAT WAS THE GREAT STINK?

No, it wasn't what historians called your bedroom after you ate that baked-bean and cauliflower casserole. It was a time when there was so much poo in the River Thames that the whole of London smelled like the inside of a horse's bum for months and months, and all the germs from it made thousands of people ill.

OI!

> It's lucky you weren't around then, or you'd have been arrested for attempted murder every day. Prunella

I'll introduce you to geniuses like Louis Pasteur, who invented pasta. No, hold on, that's not right. He worked out that infections come from germs. Before that, people used to think infections were caused by bad smells! He even worked out how to get rid of germs in food, so people didn't die from drinking manky milk.

For hundreds and hundreds of years, women weren't allowed to be doctors or scientists – a horrible example of a thing called sexism, which means treating women and men differently. Women helped millions of people by working as midwives and healers, but they never got any credit for it – or even worse, they got punished for it! I know, right . . . We'll meet some brilliant women who pushed past all that stupid sexism and changed the world, like the marvellous Marie Curie. She was the first woman to win a Nobel Prize (the top award in science), and then the first person to win a second Nobel Prize (which is slightly greedy, if you ask me). And quite right too – her discoveries still save the lives of people with cancer every single minute.

But not everyone in history was a genius. For example, there's my dad, who once destroyed his laptop by cleaning the keyboard with soapy water. Going a bit further back, we'll find out why the Ancient Egyptians thought the brain was just a useless load of old stuffing that might as well be chucked in the bin, why teachers forced their pupils to smoke cigarettes, why hairdressers would chop their customers' legs off and why people got paid for farting. (Unfortunately, that's no longer a thing – sorry.)

→ I can tell who you got your brains from. Prunella

Not gross enough for you? Well, how about the surgeons who never washed their hands and believed that the more blood and guts and brains they had on their clothes, the better? Or the ones who thought that patients should be wide awake and screaming during their operations, otherwise the surgery wouldn't be successful? Don't worry – none of them are still working today. Well, hopefully not . . .

So, if you're ready, pop a peg on your nose (there was a lot of stinky pus back then), pull on your wellies (there was a lot of poo around too), wash your hands (because *they* certainly didn't) and let's go back to where it all began. No, not dinosaurs – dinosaurs didn't have doctors. Maybe that's why they became extinct . . .

A doctor and a time machine – why has nobody ever thought of this before?! Let's go!

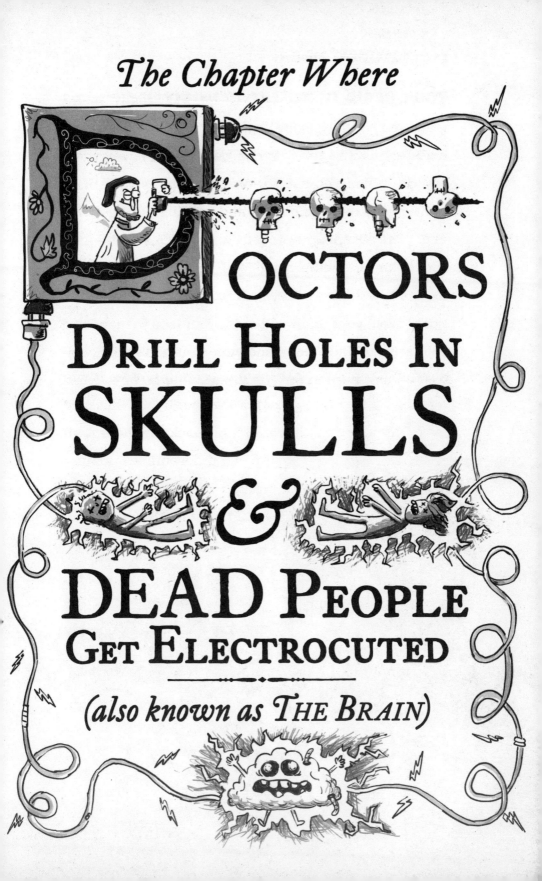

YOUR BRAIN IS, TO PUT IT MILDLY, really, really, really, really, really, really important. It's the super-smart, high-tech control centre in charge of literally everything you do. When you eat, for example: that's your brain telling your teeth to chomp and your tongue to swish and your oesophagus to . . . umm . . . oesophagize? (Oesophagus means your food pipe, btw. (And btw means 'by the way', btw.)) Need to run away from a tiger? Well, your brain will order your legs to move and your arms to flail around and your mouth to scream and your bum to fart. (Is it just me who farts when I'm scared?)

But the brain hasn't always got the respect it deserves. Years and years ago, humans were a bit slow to work it all out. Can you blame them? They didn't have the internet, for a start. Also, I hadn't written this book yet. But, if **YOU** didn't have the first clue about how the body works, would you ever really look at that big, ugly pile of slimy sausages inside your head and think, *Well, that must be the most important part of the body!*? Probably not. That's if you'd even managed to find the brain in the first place – it's securely hidden away in its secret lair, inside a big, thick lump of skull. (I mean the skull is a thick piece of bone, not that you're thick. Don't send me any emails complaining, please.)

You could say this chapter's only half written because there's loads of things we *still* don't know about the brain – even some quite major stuff, like what bits of it make us clever. In a hundred years' time, they'll probably find a copy of this book and make fun of us and how little we knew about the body.

Your poor readers. They should get a refund for this book if you don't even know how the body works. Prunella

WOW, THEY REALLY WERE IDIOTS.

ANCIENT EGYPT

Who's the oldest person you know? The oldest person I know is my Great Aunt Prunella. She's ninety-two and even **SHE** wasn't around in the time of the Ancient Egyptians. The Ancient Egyptians lived about five thousand years ago, which is nearly two million days ago, which is three billion minutes ago, which is over 150 billion seconds ago, which is a weird way to measure it, actually.

Let's start by talking about mummies, and I don't mean the people who tell you off for not eating your mushrooms or when you wipe your nose on your sleeve. I mean the kind of mummy you dress up as when you need a last-minute Halloween costume and all you can find are ten rolls of toilet paper. The Ancient Egyptians believed that, when you died, there was something called an after-life that was apparently much nicer than ordinary life (less homework and more chocolate).

How dare you tell people my age — you absolutely horrible wretch. Delete this. Prunella

To prepare important people like kings and queens for the afterlife, they mummified their bodies. I'm glad they waited until people were dead because mummification wasn't a very fun process. Priests would hopefully put some gloves on first, then remove all the person's organs, then embalm the rest of the body (which means using substances like salt to stop it going all mouldy). Just before they wrapped the body in those spooky-looking bandages, they would pop the heart back inside because they realized it was very important. Some other organs, like the lungs and the stomach, would be stored in special jars to sit alongside the body for its journey to the afterlife, a bit like hand luggage when you go on holiday.

And how about the brain? They just chucked it in the bin, mate. I'm not even joking.

The Ancient Egyptians thought cleverness came from the heart, and the brain was just a load of padding like you'd find inside a cushion, and it was only there to stop your head going all flat. So they'd yank out the brain (stop reading immediately if you're eating) by sticking a massive sharp hook up the nose (I mean it – put those cornflakes down!) and scooping it out like the world's biggest bogey, then splatting it straight in the rubbish. Then they'd shove a load of old cloth into the empty skull. Let's hope the Ancient Egyptian afterlife didn't involve spelling tests because those former royals wouldn't have done very well at all with a load of tea towels where their brains should be.

ANCIENT GREECE

It's time to take the bus to Greece (make sure you go to the loo before you leave). Ancient Greece must have been a very exciting place to live because every city was crammed full of clever people who invented all sorts of important things, such as maps and the Olympics! Unfortunately, they also invented some really annoying things like geometry (a particularly boring bit of maths) and alarm clocks (which wake you up, so you can go to school and learn maths).

They get full marks for discovering all those things, but I'm afraid they weren't too hot on the old brain stuff either. They thought the Ancient Egyptians were right and that the heart was in charge of **EVERYTHING**. And who can blame them? It's in the middle of the body, it's got blood vessels sprouting everywhere, and if you cut it out with a penknife everything else stops working. (My lawyer, Nigel, has asked me to point out that under no circumstances should you cut out your – or anyone else's – heart using a penknife.)

So what did the Ancient Greeks think the brain was for? Well, for hundreds of years, they believed it was just there to make mucus – like some kind of phlegm factory. (Maybe they saw snot leaking out of someone's nose and thought it was the brain overflowing, like a bath you forgot to turn off.) The Ancient Greeks score a D minus for that. Luckily, one day a bloke turned up who realized the brain was more than a big snot-sack, and his name was Hippocrates.

Hippocrates was one of the most important doctors of all time. In fact, he's so important that he gets his very own fact box.

HIPPOCRATES: FIVE FACTS AND A LIE

1. He's known as the Father of Medicine because of his important contributions to the subject. (Not because he had a daughter called Medicine.)

2. The Hippocratic Oath was named after him: it's something doctors in Ancient Greece had to agree to before they could start work. Doctors still do this today, although it's been changed slightly (for example, they've deleted the bit where Hippocrates said students must give their teachers money if they ask for it).

3. He was the first person to discover that what you eat and how much you exercise are

important for keeping healthy. That means he's the bloke to blame when you're forced to run outside in the cold and eat mushrooms. Ugh.

4. He wrote sixty massive books about the body – I've only written two, so that makes me feel really lazy.

5. He invented endoscopy, which is a way of looking inside the body using a tube (a bit like an empty toilet roll). Endoscopy is still used all the time by surgeons nowadays – thanks, Hippocrates!

6. He was called Hippocrates (which is Greek for Hippoface) because he had massive teeth and nostrils and looked a bit like a hippo.

NO ONE CALLS ME HIPPOFACE!

6. He wasn't really known as Hippoface, so far as we know. I guess you can call him that if you like – he's not around to tell you off. Oh, and it's pronounced hi-PO-cra-TEES, not hippo-crates.

A lot of doctors in Ancient Greece thought that illnesses were caused by magic, and Hippocrates was one of the first who reckoned that was a load of old goat poo. How would you feel if you went to the doctor because you kept falling over and they waved a magic wand over you and said 'Izzy wizzy, stop feeling dizzy!' then pulled a rabbit out of your nose? I think you might ask to see their medical certificate. But why's he in the chapter about the brain? Well, he's the super-genius who realized that the brain is responsible for doing things like thinking and feelings. Good old Hippoface!

Hippocrates died when he was about ninety, which is amazingly old for someone who lived that long ago – in fact, it's an extremely old age even now. Inventing so much medicine clearly paid off for him. Until . . . he died.

Try not to get too sad – it was over two thousand years ago. Luckily, Ancient Greece was crammed full of other clever clogs, and very soon another bearded brainiac called Aristotle came along.

ARISTOTLE: FIVE FACTS AND A LIE

1. He got a job teaching the boy who grew up to be Alexander the Great (a very famous king and soldier). I wonder what he was called when he was at school? I bet it wasn't Alexander the Great – it was probably something like Alexander Smelly Socks.

2. He invented a subject called logic, which was basically a whole new way of arguing, and he taught it to thousands of students. Imagine having arguing lessons! No, you shut up!

3. He named over five hundred different animals. (I mean he gave the names to lots of different species of animal – he didn't just keep loads of cats and say, 'You're called Floofloo, you're called Nozzle, you're called Bimpsy . . .')

4. He invented toast.

5. He guessed that Antarctica existed and gave it its name, even though he never went there (so he sadly never met a penguin).

6. He worked out that the Earth was round. Other people before him had suspected it might not be flat, but he got out his pen and paper and proved it.

4. Bread has been around for about 30,000 years, and stuff has been on fire ever since humans started wandering the Earth, so toast is a lot older than Aristotle.

Now that Hippocrates had cracked the basics of the brain, what would Aristotle add? Would he perhaps discover the functions of all the brain's separate lobes? Would he work out which bit of the brain makes us speak or dream or waggle our ears? Or . . . would he go right back to square one and say that the brain isn't important at all?

Yep, I'm afraid he undid all of Hippocrates' excellent work and convinced the whole of Ancient Greece that the heart was the only important organ and the brain was basically just a big lump of beanbag stuffing. And, because he was so famous from all his other excellent discoveries, people believed him about this as well. Drat! (Luckily, Hippocrates was dead by then, otherwise he'd have been furious.)

I guess we can't all be perfect. For example, I sometimes get my 546 times table wrong. And your head teacher has terrible dress sense. So it's fair enough that Aristotle was kind of an idiot when it came to the brain. The best explanation he could come up with was that the brain was a kind of air-conditioning system, to keep the rest of your body nice and cool. **FACT CHECK:** not remotely true.

→ Stop pretending you're so great. Do you want me to show them your school reports? Prunella

ANCIENT ROME

I'm pleased to report that Aristotle's nonsense about the brain being some kind of weird, magical fridge didn't last long. A few hundred years later, round the corner in Rome, they realized that Hippocrates probably had the right idea after all and you didn't think using your heart. Phew.

Roman scientists rolled up their togas, looked at a load of brains and spotted that there were tons of wires coming off them, and that these wires went all round the body. They said, 'These wires are nerves, and they go from the brain and tell the rest of the body what to do! Crazy!' They probably said it in Latin, but otherwise that's pretty much exactly how it happened.

Nerves were such an exciting discovery that the scientists were desperate to tell all of Ancient Rome! But how . . . ? Did they write it in a book? No – too boring. Did they make a TV programme about it? No – didn't exist. That's right – they turned it into a hideous live show. Crowds of people would go along to a big outdoor theatre, and settle down with their snacks to watch a scientist experiment on animals like lions and bears, to demonstrate how nerves worked, like some kind of horrendous circus. For example, they might cut a nerve so that an animal's voice didn't work any more. Hopefully those lions got their revenge on the scientists who did all this horrible stuff by eating them immediately after the show.

MIDDLE AGES

The next thousand years or so were known as the Middle Ages. We call them the Middle Ages because they came after one bit of history and before another bit – it's a pretty terrible name, to be honest. Makes it sound *sooooooo* boring. And it wasn't boring at all – it was full of banquets and battles, and they invented everything from gunpowder to printing and even the calendar we use today. (I mean the way we count years, not the calendar you've got up on your fridge.) Maybe I should rename the Middle Ages so they sound more exciting – this is a textbook so I guess that'll make it official. How about Sparkle Time? That sounds much better. OK, let's start this section again.

SPARKLE TIME

In Sparkle Time, they were all totally on board with the idea that the brain was a pretty important part of the body, but they still had some slightly odd ideas about how it worked. I guess these ideas felt totally sensible all those years ago, but now they just sound . . . weird. Like the haircuts your parents had when they were younger – they probably seemed fine at the time, but in photos their hair looks like an explosion in a wig factory. People in the Middle Ag– sorry, Sparkle

That's a bit rich coming from you. Your hair looks like your dog cut it. Prunella

Time thought that our brains were powered by spirits whooshing around inside them. I know, right? And they reckoned that the reason you could move your arms and legs was because these spooky little dudes would travel down your nerves (which they thought were hollow tubes) and do it for you. *Okaaaaaaay.*

How about if you had a headache, or your leg stopped working? Well, that was just the creepy brain-ghosts misbehaving. I don't want to ruin the rest of the chapter for you, but . . . nerves are nothing to do with creepy brain-ghosts.

THE KING AND EYE

BEST OF THREE?

I want you to meet Henri II of France. Well, you can't actually meet him – that would involve us all driving to France with some spades and a forklift truck because he's been dead and buried for centuries – but I want you to hear about him. Henri (which is French for Henry) II (which means the second – his surname wasn't pronounced 'eye-eye') was out one morning, enjoying his favourite hobby of jousting. Jousting involves riding on a horse and hurtling towards your opponent carrying a massive spike. A bit of a strange game, but I guess the Xbox hadn't been invented yet.

If you find yourself jousting against a king, the golden rule (if you don't want to be executed) is don't **EVER** stick the massive spike into any part of them, especially not their eye. Unfortunately, Henri's opponent, Gabriel, forgot the golden rule and . . . stuck his massive spike through the king's eye. What a **KNIGHT**mare!

This is the worst joke you've done so far – and that's saying something. Prunella

It was mostly a nightmare for King Henri, who started having terrible headaches, then his arms and legs stopped working, then he went into a coma (like a very deep sleep) and then he died. At this point, his doctors sprang into action (a tiny bit too late, if you ask me) and opened up his skull and saw what a mess his brain was in. This made them realize that even though our brains are in the middle of a big lump of bone, we have to do things ourselves to protect them. Like not jousting, and always wearing a bicycle helmet. I mean when you're cycling – you don't have to wear one in bed.

ZZZZZZZAP!

In the eighteenth century, they finally worked out that your brain sends messages down your nerves using electricity. This was big news, especially for a *dottore* (that's Italian for 'doctor' – I'm so kind, I'm teaching you languages too!) called Giovanni Aldini, who decided that he should use this exciting new discovery to . . . bring people back to life. He teamed up with a few blokes who'd had a really rubbish day. In fact, they'd just had their heads chopped off for being criminals. Aldini zapped electricity down the nerves in the dead men's spinal cords and their limbs twitched, because their arms and legs mistook this electricity for the electrical messages the brain would usually send them.

So, did these people come back to life? Well, no. Which is good because it would be pretty scary to have a bunch of headless criminals running around, smashing into you. But when a young author called Mary Shelley heard about these experiments, she was inspired to write a terrifying book about creating a monster from old body parts, using electricity to bring them to life. Do you know what it was called? That's right – *The Very Hungry Caterpillar*. Sorry, I mean *Frankenstein*.

HEADBUMPOLOGY

You know how sometimes literally **EVERYONE** is playing the same computer game or coming to school with the same gadget or toy that you absolutely must, must, must have?! And then the next minute everyone's forgotten about it and moved on to something new? This happens to adults as well – remember that exercise bike your dad used once, or the month when there was a bread maker in the kitchen?

Well, it's been going on for centuries and centuries. Two hundred years ago, everyone was into something called phrenology. Phrenology was a fancy name for when people would try to discover things about you by feeling bumps on your skull – so it should really have been called headbumpology. Phrenology fanatics thought these lumps were there because they'd been pushed out of place by super-large parts of your brain, and they claimed that by feeling your head they could tell things about your personality, or even predict the future: for example, if you were going to fall in love, or fall in a pond.

We've all got lumps on our head (go on, have a feel. Of your own, I mean – not your teacher's), but these bumpy bits have absolutely nothing to do with our brain, or our personality, or our future. In other words, phrenology was a load of poo. And not even a small load of poo, like a bird might splat on a car. I mean a **HUGE** load of poo, like if a lorry full of manure skidded on a roundabout and it all poured out and totally covered twelve houses.

→ Please can you stop writing these disgusting sentences. No one will want to read a book like this, you hideous monster. Prunella

But in those days patients couldn't just google 'Is phrenology a big load of nonsense?' so they ended up believing it. Some grown-ups weren't allowed to start a new job unless a phrenologist had scanned their scalp to see if they were trustworthy or not. Pretty bad, right?

I BELIEVE WE HAVE A JOB FOR YOU!

FINALLY!

It gets worse. Phrenologists claimed they could tell if you were a criminal, or if you were going to be one in the future, and you could even be sent to prison for it! This would have been very bad news for me because my head's bumpier than a roller coaster in an earthquake.

MENTAL HEALTH

It's very common to have problems with your mental health, and these days there are lots of people you can turn to for help. But we weren't always good at dealing with this kind of thing, to put it mildly. People wrongly believed that lots of mental health problems were caused by the moon, which is where the horrible word (that you should never use) 'lunatic' came from, because 'luna' means 'moon'. If someone had mental health problems, it was thought of as shameful – which we now know is ridiculous. Nobody today would ever be ashamed of having a broken arm or an infected tooth, and mental health problems are just like any other medical issue. But in the past, people would be sent to live in asylums.

These were awful places, and the people who lived there were treated very badly – some of the so-called cures for their illnesses basically involved beating them up or not letting them have any food. The doctors thought the shock of being treated so badly would cause any demons hiding in their body to leave. You won't be surprised to hear that this didn't work – mainly because demons aren't real. (Apologies to any demons reading this.)

To make it worse, people would even pay to come to asylums and stare at the patients – it was a top day out for them, like going to Alton Towers, except the queues were shorter at asylums and Alton Towers didn't exist in those days. Nothing like that would ever happen today, and it's really important to talk to an adult if you're ever worried about your mental health, or anyone else's.

In 1921, a German genius called Otto Loewi turned up and discovered something called neurotransmitters. You probably don't know much about neurotransmitters (unless you're Otto Loewi) but they're a **VERY** big deal. They're basically tiny chemicals that the brain uses to send messages between its cells – and too much or too little of these chemicals can affect your mental health, and how you feel and behave. Even better news came when other clever scientists developed medicines that could fix the levels of neurotransmitters in the brain.

These drugs, and talking therapies (where a trained specialist listens to problems and helps with them), meant that people with mental health problems didn't have to be locked away from the rest of the world. Obviously they shouldn't have been locked away in the first place, if you ask me, but I wasn't in charge of things then, annoyingly. One in four adults will have some kind of mental health problem every single year in the UK, so three cheers for modern treatments. Hip hip hooray! Hip hip hooray!

That's only two cheers, actually. Prunella

FANCY A SLICE OF BRAIN?

Brain surgery has been happening for a very, very long time. Brain surgery that actually **WORKS** is a much more recent invention though. Archaeologists think that brain surgery might be the first type of surgery that was ever performed. There are skulls of cavepeople born eight thousand years ago with holes drilled into them. Eight thousand years is *ages*. That's enough time to watch seventy million episodes of your favourite TV show. Although you might get bored after a few million.

The whole drilling-into-heads idea stuck around for centuries and was done for all sorts of reasons, from curing headaches to letting out evil spirits (which didn't exist in the first place). It even had a fancy name: trepanning. It was so common that in some graveyards they've found that more than one in ten people had holes drilled into their skulls. (My lawyer, Nigel, has asked me to point out that it's extremely important that you don't drill a hole into anyone's skull.)

AT LEAST YOUR HEADACHES HAVE CLEARED UP.

While over here in Europe we took a long time to come up with surgery any more complicated than that, in India they were miles ahead of the game. Over a thousand years ago, a king of India called Raja Bhoja was having terrible headaches, which his doctors thought might be caused by a lump in his brain. Not only was their diagnosis right, but they were able to cut into his skull to remove this lump – and he was totally cured! He went on to massively expand his kingdom, compose music and write about eighty books. Honestly, why did all these people write so many books? It makes me feel like such an underachiever.

Their books were probably a lot better than the rubbish you write too. Prunella

But not everyone was getting it right. In fact, a lot of what we've learned about the brain over the centuries comes from mistakes that happened during brain surgery. About seventy years ago, an American man called Henry Molaison was having terrible seizures, which means his body kept shaking. His doctors thought they could cure Henry's condition by removing part of his brain. Can you guess the slight problem with this plan? What if that part of the brain was . . . important? As it turns out, the bit the doctors removed was **EXTREMELY** important and, after the surgery, Henry suddenly couldn't make any new memories. If you told him something one day (or even splatted a cake in his face), he wouldn't remember it at all the next day. This was pretty bad news for Henry, but it meant that for the first time scientists knew which part of the brain was responsible for memories. When he died in 2008, his brain was sliced into thousands of tiny bits and every single piece was photographed and put on the internet. Interesting for scientists, I suppose, but to me it sounds like the most boring Instagram account ever. If my brain gets chopped up, I'd like the slices to be used as miniature frisbees.

BRAINFLIX

Dreams are pretty strange – they're like this TV show that happens in your own head while you're asleep – so it's not surprising that there have been some really weird explanations for them over the years. The Ancient Egyptians thought dreams were messages from the gods – and they'd even sleep in special dream-beds to encourage the gods to send them these magical WhatsApps. Other people throughout history thought that dreams were a way of predicting the future. King Xerxes of Persia kept having a dream that his army should invade Greece, so . . . he did.

This went very badly wrong, which goes to show that you shouldn't just do things that happen while you're zzzz-ing. That's a big shame because I have this dream where I live in a house made of chocolate buttons and marshmallows, and it sounds dead fun. Anyway, the truth is that dreams aren't messages from gods or predictions about the future. They're much more boring than that – it's just your brain storing away things it learned during the day.

THE FUTURE

I'm sure your robot butler has got all the standard modules built in, like window washing, pizza cooking and cleaning dog poo off the carpet (thank goodness). I've just upgraded mine so he's now got a future-prediction module, and can tell us what medicine's going to look like in the years to come.

PREDICTION 1 — PATIENTS WILL BE ABLE TO BEAM INSTRUCTIONS FROM THEIR BRAIN USING A NEURAL CONTROL INTERFACE.

Cool! I don't know about you, but I've always fancied being able to beam my thoughts into other people's heads. I'd be able to order a takeaway using my mind, or tell my dog, Pippin, to stop licking up that vomit she found on the pavement by sending her my *UGH STOP NO* brainwaves. (She'd probably still ignore me though.)

I don't know why they'd use such a boring-sounding name as Neural Control Interface for something so brilliant. I'd have called it the Brainwave Utilization Machine (or BUM).

Imagine being able to control machines using only your thoughts? Or downloading all your homework on to your computer directly out of your brain in one second? (You should probably check through it very carefully though, in case your brain was also busy thinking about how boring your teacher is.) Best of all, this technology could mean that people who are paralysed might be able to use their arms or legs in the future. Amazing!

PREDICTION 2 — YOU'RE HAVING PASTA FOR DINNER TONIGHT.

Oh, lovely! No mushrooms, thanks.

ADAM'S ANSWERS

HOW DID DOCTORS DISCOVER WHICH PART OF THE BRAIN CONTROLS YOUR PERSONALITY?

By accident! In 1848, a man called Phineas Gage had a really bad shift at work. He was on a building site, making a new railway when – *BOOM!* – a massive explosion caused a huge metal pole to shoot all the way through his skull. Oops. Amazingly, he survived, even though the pole smooshed through a big chunk of his brain. One thing was very different though – his personality had totally changed from kind and charming (like me) to rude and moany (like you). This made scientists realize that the part of his brain that was damaged, known as the frontal lobe, had something to do with personality.

HOW DID A RECORD COMPANY HELP US UNDERSTAND THE BRAIN?

In the 1960s, a man called Godfrey Hounsfield was working at EMI, a company that made records for some of the biggest pop stars in the world, like the Beatles, the Beach Boys, and other bands that didn't begin with the letter B. Godfrey worked in the computer department there and one day clearly got a bit bored and wondered to himself if there was any way of doing a scan that looked inside the brain. A lot of fiddling and a bunch of experiments (on himself) later, he invented the CT scanner, which uses X-ray technology to show slices of any part of the body. It's still one of the main ways doctors look at the brain today.

WHY DO SOME PEOPLE HAVE THEIR HEADS FROZEN AFTER THEY DIE?

What a cheery question! Well, seeing as you asked, for the last fifty years, some people have believed in cryonics, which means freezing their chopped-off head after they die. The idea is that in the future, when science has got much more advanced, they can be brought back to life and their heads glued on to robot bodies or kept in a big jar or something. Unfortunately for these people, scientists are pretty certain there's never going to be any way to wake them up because all this does so much damage to the brain. Freezers are for ice creams, not heads.

TRUE OR POO?

OUR BRAINS ARE BIGGER THAN THOSE OF OUR ANCESTORS.

POO Yep, sorry about this. I know you probably think grown-ups are idiots (and, to be fair, a lot of them are), but their brains are actually bigger than yours – brains have slowly been getting smaller for thousands of years. And no, it's not because of all the TV you watch or because you don't eat your vegetables. Scientists don't actually know why it's happening, but the good news is that a smaller brain doesn't mean we're any less clever. In fact, smaller brains are often quicker at thinking, like a speedy little sports car is faster than a big old bin lorry.

DOCTORS TRIED TO TREAT MENTAL ILLNESS BY PULLING PATIENTS' TEETH OUT.

TRUE Horrifically, this didn't even happen a particularly long time ago – less than a hundred years in fact. Some doctors thought that mental illness was caused by infections hiding somewhere in the body, and they'd remove whatever they thought might have some lurgy lurking inside. Teeth, tonsils, stomachs and intestines would all get whipped out. Obviously it didn't help in the slightest, and over half of these poor people died as a result.

DOCTORS USED ELECTRICITY TO TREAT PAIN TWO THOUSAND YEARS AGO.

TRUE I'd forgive you for thinking this was an absolute load of poo because we didn't work out how to make electricity until about a couple of hundred years ago. But, thousands of years ago, doctors realized they could help pain in a patient's feet by pressing an electric eel on them. (That's right – they put eels onto heels.) Doctors still use electricity as a kind of pain relief today, but no slimy sea snakes are required.

I GET ALL THE WORST JOBS.

CRAZY CURES

If you're upset that the person you fancy doesn't like you back, then you should probably just have a massive tub of popcorn and forget about them. In Sparkle Time (fine, the Middle Ages), your doctor would have had a different plan:

STEP ONE: get hold of a poo done by the person you fancy. (This is the trickiest part.)

STEP TWO: set fire to their poo. (This is the most dangerous part.)

STEP THREE: breathe in all the pooey fumes. (This is the most disgusting part.)

STEP FOUR: the person you like will immediately fall in love with you. (This is the most unlikely part.)

(My lawyer, Nigel, has requested that you don't read the Crazy Cures sections at the end of each chapter.)

The Chapter With

BLOOD-SUCKING
LEECHES
&
A SMOKING
BUMHOLE

(also known as CIRCULATION)

BY THE TIME YOU FINISH THIS SENTENCE, every single drop of blood you have will have gone on a complete circuit of your body. And – how about that? – it's gone all the way round again already. Your heart pumps blood through your arteries, and then the blood pops back to your heart through your veins, before whizzing off to your lungs to get some more scrumptious oxygen . . . and then the whole process starts again. I'm sure you know this already (or at least you should pretend to, if a teacher asks), but how did we get to knowing all this from knowing absolutely none of it?

Even though it took humans **AGES** to realize that the brain was anything more than a bunch of squidgy skull-stuffing, we've known the heart was useful for zillions of years (well, not quite zillions). It might have taken a bit of a while to figure out **EXACTLY** how it all worked in there, but we've known it was pretty crucial for the whole 'being alive' thing ever since we wore jeans made out of mammoth fur.

How did they know this so long ago? Well, let's imagine a sabre-toothed tiger decided to chomp off a bit of a caveperson for lunch. If it fancied an arm or an ear, that was pretty annoying for Mr Caveman, but it didn't mean it was time to measure him up for a coffin just yet. However, if our pointy-fanged friend thought the caveman's heart looked particularly tasty, it was definitely game over: no heart equals no life. Mrs Cavewoman would probably be quite upset, but Dr Caveperson would be thinking, *Hmm – that part of the body seems pretty important. Ugg.*

Luckily, there was still a little bit more to discover about the heart than that, otherwise this chapter would be extremely short. ⟶ *That's a shame — I wish this book was over already. Pranella*

ANCIENT EGYPT

Have you ever been given credit for something you didn't actually do? Like if your sister tidied the living room and you pretended that you did it? Well, for thousands of years, the heart got the credit for almost everything that happened in the body. The Ancient Egyptians noticed there were tubes coming off the heart going in all sorts of different directions, so they decided that it was responsible for moving around blood (yep!), spit (umm, nope), poo (what were they thinking?), the soul (is that even a thing?) and ghosts (umm, guys . . .).

But, to be fair to the Ancient Egyptians, they were the first people to realize that the pulse they could feel in people's wrists told them how fast the heart was beating. They also spotted that when people fainted their pulses often got slower and harder to find, and that some illnesses made the heart get bigger and not work as well. Still doesn't make up for the whole 'poo goes through the heart' thing though.

You might remember that if you were important and royal enough to get turned into a mummy, then you'd have your heart plopped back into your body before you got wrapped up in kitchen roll. But getting into the afterlife wasn't as simple as that – the Ancient Egyptians believed the gods had to give a test first. *What sort of test?* you might wonder . . . Singing 'Happy Birthday' backwards in German? Swimming through a crocodile-infested swamp? Nope – the gods would weigh a person's heart and if it weighed more than a feather, then they wouldn't be allowed in. The Ancient Egyptian afterlife must have had hardly anybody in it – hearts weigh a lot more than a feather: they're usually as heavy as a big potato.

> It's a bit pathetic if they don't remember – it was literally a few pages ago. Prunella

ANCIENT GREECE

Time to see what Aristotle made of the heart. Surely he could have a better guess about what it does other than pushing poo and spit round the body? Well, not really. He thought it sent air whooshing through your nerves and moved all your muscles, like the body was some kind of weird puppet. Very imaginative, but total drivel. And it turns out he wasn't very good at maths – he cut open a heart and claimed it had three chambers in it, even though it's got four. He's meant to be this super-genius, but he couldn't even count to four. Honestly.

And you're some kind of genius, are you? I know for a fact that you can't tie your shoelaces. Prunella

YOU'VE WON THE CLEVEREST PERSON AWARD AGAIN.

HIGH FOUR!

According to Aristotle, there wasn't much old hearty couldn't do. He reckoned it was in charge of all your thoughts and feelings, and was also a heater that kept the body going – like a massive fleshy radiator. Even weirder, he thought the cleverer you were, the more heat your heart would produce. Imagine if you wrote any of this in your science exam? They'd kick you out of school and make you wear a T-shirt that said I AM AN IDIOT.

I should get you one of those for Christmas. Prunella

ANCIENT ROME

You might be wondering why these people kept getting it wrong for hundreds of years. Well, in Ancient Rome, it was totally against the law for scientists to cut into the body of someone who'd died. Instead, they cut open dogs, pigs and monkeys, and just assumed that all creatures had the same inner workings. As you might have guessed, humans aren't the same as dogs. (I'm glad I'm not the same as Pippin, otherwise I'd spend all day eating slippers and rolling around in fox poo.) If humans and dogs really did have the same insides, you'd be able to go to the vets to get your broken arm fixed – and you'd never be able to eat a Twix because chocolate makes dogs really ill.

But, despite all this, the Ancient Romans did work out some important things about the heart – mostly thanks to a man called Galen.

PIPPUS MAXIMUS

FOXUS POOUS

GALEN: FIVE FACTS AND A LIE

1. He wrote his first textbook when he was thirteen. So I hope you're planning to write one pretty soon . . .

2. The books he wrote contained over **TEN MILLION** words. That's more than ten times longer than everything lazy Shakespeare wrote (and two hundred times longer than this book).

3. One night, Galen's dad had a dream that said Galen should study medicine instead of philosophy, so Daddy Galen forced him.

4. His full name was Galen Xalen.

5. He was head doctor to the gladiators. (There wasn't much for him to do – you can't really help someone who's been turned into a human kebab by their opponent's sword.)

NEXT!

6. He invented a type of eye surgery that is still performed today.

4. We don't actually know his surname, only that his first name was Galen. Maybe he was one of those people who just have one name, like Adele or Pink or God.

When it came to his discoveries about the heart, Galen either got things absolutely correct, or totally and utterly wrong.

He realized there were two different types of blood vessel in the body: arteries and veins. **CORRECT!** Well done, Galen!

He said that the heart isn't a muscle. **NONSENSE!** Bad Galen! (It's the most important muscle in the body.)

He spotted that the blood in the arteries is much brighter than the blood in the veins. **CORRECT!** Have a gold star, Galen! (It's because there's a lot more oxygen in the blood in the arteries compared with the veins.)

He thought that, when blood goes off to a part of the body, it gets gobbled up, so you have to eat some food to make more blood. **NONSENSE!** Swap that gold star for a poo-coloured one. (Blood flows around the body in a circle – down through the arteries and back through the veins – that's why it's called circulation, you see.)

Galen's books must have been extremely convincing and well written because everyone totally believed him. Trouble was, quite a lot of the time he just . . . guessed. That's not great, is it? Well, it — gets worse – no one questioned his ideas for more than a thousand years!

Unlike yours, then. Prunella

SPARKLE TIME

In Sparkle Time (which some losers call the Middle Ages), a doctor in Syria started to wonder if Galen's heart theory wasn't quite right after all. Finally! He was called Ala-al-Din abu al-Hasan Ali ibn Abi-Hazm al-Qarshi al-Dimashqi, but he was also known as Ibn al-Nafis – probably because Ala-al-Din abu al-Hasan Ali ibn Abi-Hazm al-Qarshi al-Dimashqi didn't fit on the sign on his door.

Like a lot of brainboxes in those days, Ibn al-Nafis wasn't just a doctor – he was an expert in all sorts of things, including law and astronomy. It's good to have a backup career, I suppose. I'm not sure how Ibn al-Nafis had any time to see patients because he also wrote over a hundred books. (Once – just once – I'd like to be able to tell you about some doctor from the past who only wrote two books. I'd feel a lot better about myself then.)

In around 1250, Ibn al-Nafis totally worked out circulation. He realized the heart was connected to the lungs, that there are tiny vessels called capillaries between the veins and arteries, and he counted the number of chambers in the heart correctly. Hooray – bring out the party poppers! Unfortunately, Ibn al-Nafis' discoveries were soon forgotten about, and everyone went straight back to Galen's terrible ideas. Boo – put the party poppers away again.

It wasn't until 1924 that someone found one of his books and went, 'Whoops, this bloke worked it all out ages ago!'

You might have spotted that all the doctors a long time ago were men. That's not because women didn't want to be doctors, and it's not because women weren't just as good at medicine. It's because it was against the (extremely stupid) law. The church was worried that if too many people got cured by medicine then they would stop believing in prayer, so they said that any woman who healed someone was a witch and needed to be arrested. But this still didn't stop lots of wonderful women from helping patients. In 1322, a woman called

Jacobina Félicie was put on trial in France for 'illegally' being a doctor. She called lots of her patients as witnesses, who said that she was much better than any of the male doctors in Paris. But she was still found guilty – ridiculous!

WILLIAM HARVEY

Let's fast-forward to the 1600s. Isaac Newton is busy discovering gravity by getting donked on the head by apples, Galileo is staring up into the sky to work out what the planets are up to, and Shakespeare is sitting at his desk, writing boring plays. Meanwhile, William Harvey was starting to wonder if Galen's theories were a load of nonsense. He thought it didn't sound quite right that your body immediately used up all the blood that flowed through it and you then had to make new blood out of food: if that was true, then everyone would have to eat about eight hundred hamburgers every lunchtime to stay alive. Nobody eats that much (if you're having eight hundred hamburgers for lunch, I strongly advise you to cut down) and we don't all collapse because we've run out of blood, so he proved that Galen was making it all up. So that's a custard pie in the face for Galen.

You can talk! This whole book is garbage. Prunella

WILLIAM HARVEY: FIVE FACTS AND A LIE

1. He lived in a huge treehouse in an oak at the bottom of his garden, so he could spend more time looking at wildlife.

2. He was the head doctor of a big hospital in London, and earned a salary of £33 per year. (That's the cost of four tins of Quality Street, so I hope chocolate was much cheaper then.)

3. He learned about the body by cutting people open, including his dad and his sister. (My lawyer, Nigel, asks me to mention that you shouldn't cut open any members of your family – however annoying they are.)

4. He saved the lives of lots of women who were on trial for being witches. He would cut up their supposedly magical toads in court to prove they were just standard boring toads, and so the women couldn't be witches.

I'M NOT A BIG FAN OF THIS BLOKE, TO BE HONEST.

5. He became King James I's doctor, and his job title at the palace was Physician Extraordinary.

6. Loads of his discoveries were lost forever when his library was destroyed in the Great Fire of London in 1666. (He should have photocopied it – honestly, back up your work, Harvs.)

1. That's absolute rubbish, sorry. He lived in a normal, non-tree-based house.

As well as sussing out circulation, Harvey also realized why our veins have **VALVES** in them, which was previously a bit of a mystery. It's so the blood only flows in one direction, otherwise it would all end up sloshing back down our legs, and instead of feet we would have enormous balloons filled with blood.

He was so nervous about writing his discoveries down in a book that he didn't tell anyone about them for thirteen years. Why was he nervous? Maybe he was worried his handwriting wasn't neat enough and that everyone would make fun of him? Or perhaps he thought no one would buy his book because it didn't have enough jokes in it and his bedroom would end up full of boxes of unsold copies? Nope – in the past, people who suggested Galen might be wrong found themselves burned at the stake (seriously!) and Willz was in no hurry to get himself barbecued.

→ *like yours? Prunella*

RESTARTY HEARTY

Let's talk about cardiopulmonary resuscitation, or CPR as we call it if we're in a hurry. And if someone needs CPR then you're definitely in a hurry because it means their heart isn't beating properly. Eek. You've probably seen it on TV before, or maybe you've been taught it at school – it involves pressing down on the chest to get the heart working and sometimes breathing into the person's lungs to give them oxygen. Presumably, as soon as doctors figured out circulation, they immediately invented CPR . . . Of course they didn't!

In fact, they got it really, really, really, really, really (please imagine another six thousand 'really's here) wrong. Instead of breathing into someone's mouth, they thought the answer was blowing smoke up their bumhole. Stop laughing – this is a serious textbook.

About three hundred years ago, if someone collapsed, then doctors would get a set of bellows (basically an old-school hand-operated pump) and a tube for . . . well, sticking up the bum. They'd then fill it with smoke and pump away. If that didn't work, they would blow smoke right into the person's mouth. I really hope they cleaned the tube first.

Strangest of all, this didn't only happen inside hospitals. Just like we now have defibrillators (machines that can restart people's hearts) in public places, back then they had these smoke-bum-pumps on the streets, just in case anyone collapsed outside.

→ This book is meant to be for children! Delete this whole section or you'll be sent to prison. And good riddance to you. Prunella

And did it work? What do you think?!

1651

A young man called
Hugh Montgomery was in
a horrible accident, smashing
open his skin and ribs, so that you
could literally see his heart beating away
(unless he was wearing a shirt, obviously).
Somehow, Hugh was OK after this, and lots
of people were keen to have a look (yuck)
or even to touch it (double yuck), including
William Harvey and even King Charles I.

EAR WE GO

You know the stethoscope – the Y-shaped thingamy doctors use to listen to your heart and your lungs and your other bits? The thing that makes you jump up twenty metres in the air because it's **SO COLD** when it touches your skin? (I would put mine in the freezer to use on patients I didn't like . . .)

Back in 1816, there was a French doctor called René-Théophile-Hyacinthe Laennec, or René to his friends. In those days, doctors didn't have any stethoscopes around their necks (or in their freezers) so, if they wanted to listen to the heart or the lungs, they'd have to just push their ear right up against the patient's skin. One day, René thought, *Well, that's a bit weird and disgusting, isn't it?* (in French) and decided to roll up a newspaper to listen to the patient's chest through that. *Blimey!* he thought (in French again) because he was suddenly able to hear the sounds much more clearly than before.

He must have reckoned that rolled-up newspaper didn't look professional enough, so he toddled off to his flute-making workshop (his hobby was making flutes – get a better hobby, mate). He made a tube from wood and metal, kind of like a really wide flute, and – hey presto! – the world's first stethoscope.

REPLACING THE RED STUFF

I'm not spilling any big medical secrets if I tell you that if you don't have enough blood in your body (for example, if you lose a lot in an accident or in an operation) then it can be extremely serious. Doctors have been attempting to replace lost blood since William Harvey's time. They've used all sorts of things to top up the body's blood supply, including beer, wine, milk, dog's blood and (in case you thought any of these ideas weren't ridiculous enough) wee. Unsurprisingly, none of these worked. At all.

If you don't stop talking about these fluids, then I will be writing to your mother. Prunella

ON SECOND THOUGHTS . . . DO YOU DO WEE?

1956

Wilson Greatbatch invented a portable device that people could put on their chest to measure their heartbeat. Unfortunately, he made it slightly wrong and it ended up giving out electric shocks every second or two. No good at all for measuring heartbeats, but amazing for giving a regular heartbeat to people whose tickers can't tick properly on their own. He called it the pacemaker, and these days three million people in the world are walking around with pacemakers in their hearts. Not bad for something invented by accident!

In 1818, a doctor called James Blundell was called to see a woman who had lost lots of blood after having a baby. *I know!* he thought. *I'll replace the blood she's lost with some from her husband*, and he got to work, hooking them up together with tubes. Success! And, because taking-blood-from-one-person-and-giving-it-to-another was a bit tricky to say, this became known as a transfusion.

Very happy with his new miracle cure, he started using this method on lots of patients who'd lost blood. Unfortunately, it wasn't as big a miracle as he'd hoped – half his patients died from it. Oops. Exactly why this happened remained a bit of a mystery until nearly a hundred years later when, in 1900, Karl Landsteiner worked out that different people have different blood types. We now know that (if you want to stay alive) you need to have a transfusion of the same type of blood that you already have – otherwise it's like filling a car up with milk instead of petrol.

SQUIDGY SURGERY

If smoke started pouring out of my car, I'd probably open up the bonnet, stare inside for a few minutes, wondering what to do . . . and then close it again because it's way too complicated in there. That's how doctors felt about the heart for thousands of years. They thought it was impossible to operate on, and assumed that if they tried, it would result in a very dead patient and a very cross hospital cleaner, because there'd be blood all over the walls and the floor and the ceiling.

It wasn't until 1896 that a doctor called Ludwig Rehn did the first heart surgery, on a man who was extremely broken-hearted. And, by broken-hearted, I don't mean that he was sad. No, someone had stabbed him in the heart with a knife. Ludwig thought, *Well, if I don't do anything, he'll die*, so he got out his needle and thread and saved the patient's life. Today, over half a million open-heart operations are performed every single year and, yep, open-heart surgery is exactly what it sounds like – they open up the heart. Yuck.

LEECH TO THEIR OWN

For about two thousand years, if you went to the doctor about almost anything, the chances were they'd suggest bloodletting. *Letting your blood do what?* you might wonder. Answer: letting your blood slosh out of you and down the sink. That's right – they thought lots of problems were caused by having too much blood. Headache? Get rid of some blood. Fainted? Bloodletting time. A touch of the plague? *Splish splash splosh*. Whose idea was this? I'm not sure, but it sounds like something a vampire would come up with.

Different doctors had different ways of doing their bloodletting, some would use massive machetes and others would use sharp scalpels. And some would strap the patient into a special chair and let bloodsucking creatures called leeches get to work with their ugly, toothy jaws. One hospital in Manchester used over 50,000 leeches in a single year! And the Ancient Egyptians thought that leeches were a really good cure for farting. ⟶ *It's just as well you weren't around in those days — I've smelled your bedroom! Prunella*

Happily, bloodletting was a massive success and every single person who had it done was cured almost immediately. No, that's not quite right, actually. Bloodletting was a total disaster and literally millions of people died because of it.

WE NEED TO GET YOU TO A DOCTOR!

BUT I'VE JUST BEEN!

So why did they keep doing it for so long? No idea, really. I guess they didn't have any other options. Or, obviously, they could have all been vampires.

OK, quick quiz. What links the following people: Pope Innocent VIII, King Charles II, Queen Anne, Mozart and President George Washington?

1. They were all in a pop group called the Beatles.
2. They all died after bloodletting.
3. They all ate swan's eggs for breakfast.

Here's a clue: this is the section about bloodletting. (It was 2. They all died after bloodletting.)

Luckily, as soon as doctors came up with actual cures for diseases, bloodletting became about as popular as jumping out of a plane without a parachute. But it took a long time for this to happen – in 1935, a medical textbook was still recommending bloodletting as a cure for things like asthma, infections and even sunstroke. Weirdly, leeches have come back into fashion though, and these days some doctors use them to help wounds heal. Cool, but also . . . yuck.

THE FUTURE

Now it's back to my robot butler, who has just made me a knickerbocker glory. (Unfortunately, he used actual knickers.)

> **PREDICTION 1 — REPLACEMENT HEARTS WILL BE 3D-PRINTED.**

White-coat-wearing geniuses are currently working on this, using tissue taken from pigs. Before too long (but hopefully after this book comes out, otherwise I'll look like an idiot) it should be possible to make a brand-new heart from scratch in a lab, for people whose hearts have stopped working properly. This will be amazing, life-changing news for patients who are on a waiting list for a heart transplant. (My lawyer, Nigel, has asked me to mention that 3D-printing a heart using pig cells is much harder than it sounds, so you shouldn't try this at home by shoving a couple of sausages into your printer.)

> **PREDICTION 2 — CHRISTMAS WILL BE ON DECEMBER 25TH THIS YEAR.**

That's not a particularly impressive prediction, to be honest.

ADAM'S ANSWERS

WHEN DID DOCTORS STOP BLOODLETTING?

They're still doing it! I know I said that it didn't have the best success rate at treating patients (thanks to its tendency to kill them), but bloodletting has made a bit of a comeback. It's only used for a couple of conditions though, such as polycythaemia, where your body makes too many red blood cells. (These days, they take the blood out very carefully, using a syringe: nobody's bleeding into a bowl.)

WHEN WAS THE FIRST HEART TRANSPLANT PERFORMED?

The first heart transplant was performed by a doctor called James Hardy in 1964 on a man whose heart had stopped working properly. Dr Hardy decided to replace it with a chimpanzee's heart and this . . . didn't work . . . at all. Three years later, in 1967, Dr Christiaan Barnard performed the first transplant, using a human heart, which was a lot more successful. It went so well, in fact, that heart transplants now save the lives of thousands of people every single year.

HOW MUCH BLOOD CAN A LEECH DRINK IN A SINGLE MEAL?

About ten millilitres, which is a couple of teaspoons. It might not sound much, but that's about ten times its own weight. (I'm the same when I'm at an all-you-can-eat buffet, to be honest.)

COOL! INFINITE REFILLS!

TRUE OR POO?

DRINKING BLOOD WAS A POPULAR TREATMENT IN ANCIENT ROME.

TRUE It didn't work, obviously, but they thought you could cure diseases such as epilepsy by having a delicious cup of warm blood. They reckoned the best blood to drink was from criminals, for some gross reason. Again, they could have been vampires, I guess.

PEOPLE WERE ALWAYS BURIED WITH THEIR HEARTS INSIDE THEIR BODIES.

POO In Sparkle Time (which I hope is what you're calling the Middle Ages by now), lots of people were buried with their heart in a different place to the rest of their body. Why have one funeral when you can have two, I guess? Some people wanted their body buried in the same graveyard as their family, but their heart to go in a place that meant a lot to them while they were alive. (I'd probably have my heart buried in the car park of my local Chinese restaurant.) There was another, slightly more disgusting reason why this happened: if someone died in battle miles and miles from home, their heart would be taken back home in a jar to keep it fresh, but their body would have to be left behind, otherwise it would decompose on the journey. And nobody wants their luggage covered in corpse juice, do they?

A DOCTOR WON A NOBEL PRIZE FOR OPERATING ON HIS OWN HEART.

TRUE In 1929, a German doctor called Werner Forssmann worked out a method of putting a tube directly into the heart, using a vein in his arm. He thought (correctly) that inserting a tube into the heart would be very useful for delivering certain types of drugs, but nobody had tried it before, and he was worried that it might instantly kill the person. So, instead of trying it out on a patient, he had a go on himself. And he immediately died. No! Come back! Stop crying! I'm joking – he was fine. It's a procedure that is still used all the time. (My lawyer, Nigel, advises you very strongly not to do any medical experiments on yourself, especially not on your heart. There is no guarantee that someone will award you a Nobel Prize for it.)

CRAZY CURES

In Ancient Egypt, they were big fans of the red stuff. Hair going grey? What you need is a lovely blood shampoo. Got an infection? Have a relaxing dip in a bright red bath of blood. Honestly, hadn't they heard of antibiotics? (Well, no, actually.)

THAT'S DISGUSTING. I'M TRYING TO HAVE A NICE RELAXING BLOOD BATH!

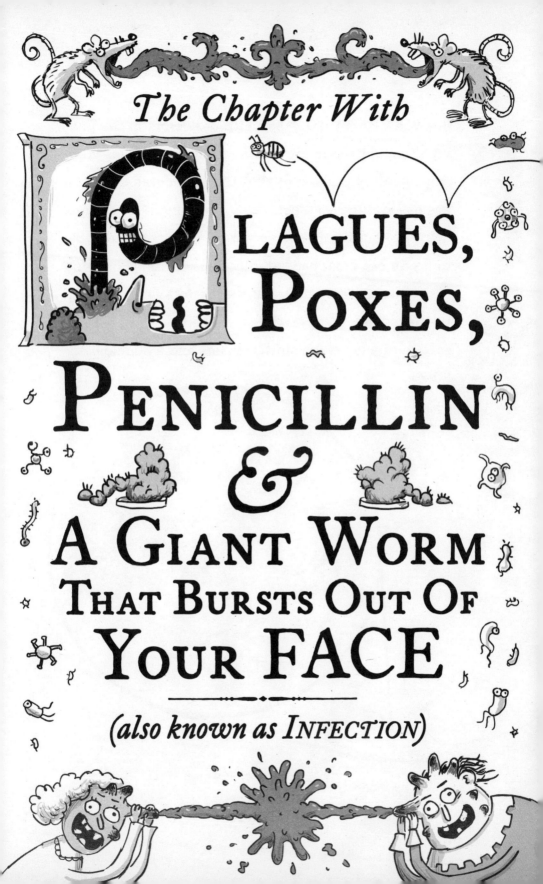

The Chapter With

PLAGUES, POXES, PENICILLIN & A GIANT WORM THAT BURSTS OUT OF YOUR FACE

(also known as INFECTION)

I'M VERY HAPPY TO MAKE FUN of doctors in the past who thought the heart was a radiator, or nerves were controlled by ghosts, or that the brain was a load of useless stuffing – in fact, I've spent hundreds of pages doing it – but I can't be cross at them for not being able to figure out what caused infections, because bacteria and viruses are so tiny that they're totally invisible to the naked eye. (Why do we say 'naked eye'? It's not like eyes normally wear a shirt, trousers and a bobble hat.)

So, before microscopes were invented and doctors discovered these microscopic meanies, how did they deal with infections? Well, other than extremely badly. Let's find out. Or, if you couldn't care less, skip to the next chapter.

I think I'll do that. Prunella

MESOPOTAMIA

No, I haven't just made up a word. And no, it's not a part of the body, or a kind of soup – it's a place. Yes, I know you've never seen an advert for a weekend break in Mesopotamia. Yes, I know you've never watched an episode of *Mesopotamia's Got Talent*. But countries change their names over time. New York used to be called New Amsterdam and France used to be Gaul, and the place we now call Iraq used to be known as Mesopotamia.

You know how you sometimes have a really good idea, but no one listens to you, and you were totally right all along? Like when I had the brainwave that mushrooms should be made illegal, so I wrote to the government telling them to do it, and they totally ignored me, and now mushrooms are still being served up at dinner for people every day, even though they're totally disgusting and probably poisonous.

Well, back in 500 BC, doctors in Mesopotamia worked out the basics of infection. They didn't know about bacteria and viruses yet, but they did realize that if someone had an infection and you locked them away, then no one else would catch it.

They even realized that wounds healed faster if doctors washed their hands in a mixture of honey, alcohol and myrrh – basically the world's first hand wash. Amazing! Except . . . this all got totally ignored and forgotten about for thousands of years. Instead, doctors came along who decided that infections were either some kind of punishment from the gods, or bad air wafting around, or the body being taken over by evil ghosts. Sigh.

ANCIENT EGYPT

If you lived in Ancient Egypt, then you probably had a pet that you took around everywhere with you. Not a dog like Pippin who licks her own bum and then licks my face (ugh). Or even a pet like a baboon or a crocodile. No, a worm. The problem with this particular pet was you couldn't put it on a lead, or pose for selfies with it. Why? Because, unfortunately, it lived inside your body! Water in those days was contaminated with tiny worm eggs that would hatch inside whoever drank it, and then grow to about thirty centimetres long, which is about the length of a ruler (I mean a school ruler, not someone like Henry VIII or Tutankhamun). Eventually, these worms would decide it was time to make their way out

of the body. Phew. But they didn't just get pooed out –
they liked to burrow their way right through the body
and burst out of places like the skin on someone's leg or
the corner of their eye. Yuck, that's disgusting. I think I
need to go in the garden now to get some fresh air – see
you in a minute. Oh no. I saw a worm when I was in the
garden and it reminded me of the ones that burst from
people's eye sockets.

If doctors saw a worm coming out of someone, then they
would wrap it round a twig, and twist it again and again
until it all squirmed out – like you'd wind spaghetti
round a fork. Thankfully, this kind of worm infestation is
now pretty rare, but there are still a few cases of it every
year. Sleep well!

SPARKLE TIME

I don't know if there's a prize for the most terrifying-sounding illness, but the Black Death has to be right up there, doesn't it? I mean it's got the word 'death' in it, for a start.

One day in 1347 a bunch of ships rocked up in Italy and all the sailors on it were either dead or covered in horrible pus-filled boils. The people standing on the harbour screamed, *'Aaaagh!'* (which is Italian for *'Aaaagh!'*), but it was too late because rats had already scampered off the ship, and those rats had fleas on them, and those fleas had plague-causing bacteria on them.

When someone became infected, they'd get a really high fever and big black swellings in their armpits or neck (hence the 'black' bit of the name), and then their fingers and toes would rot away, and then they'd vomit up blood, go into a coma and die (hence the 'death' bit of the name). Generally pretty unpleasant, I think you'll agree. You should never moan about having a slight sniffle ever again.

The Black Death swept through Europe, killing tens of millions of people: more than a third of the population. The main problem was that no one had worked out why it was spreading. Their best guess was that God had sent the plague to punish them, so they spent a lot of time trying to pray it away, or punishing themselves by whipping their own backs. They also lit lots of massive fires in an attempt to burn the bad air they thought was causing the disease. Unfortunately, none of this worked.

Eventually, the plague died out because of an idea called quarantine. If someone arrived in a country from somewhere else, they'd have to stay inside for forty days and would only be allowed out if they didn't develop the illness in that time. The word quarantine comes from *quaranta*, which is the Italian word for 'forty'. Next time an adult uses the word quarantine, see if they know that. (If they don't, then you're allowed to call them a massive ninny and make them sit in the corner for forty minutes.) Quarantine is still used, and it still works – it was one of the main ways that countries were able to control the coronavirus pandemic.

Like that terrible band whose music your parents always play in the car, the plague kept coming back out of retirement for one last tour. It reappeared loads of times over the next few hundred years, including the Great Plague of London in 1665. It wasn't that great, to be honest – if you ask me, it was actually pretty rubbish. All the rich people (including the king) fled London to their big homes in the country, so the plague mostly affected the poorer people who were left behind. Throughout history, and even to this day, it's a very sad fact that the people in the world who have the least suffer the most from illnesses.

BIG TISSUE!

I ♥ LONDON

I ♥ LONDON

Plague doctors plodded around London, offering totally useless treatments like bloodletting. There were two reasons they only offered useless treatments: firstly, there weren't any antibiotics yet; and secondly, they weren't even proper doctors – they were basically just blokes wandering about in terrifying costumes. They wore a black hat, a black cape and a mask like a pigeon's head with a really long beak that they put strong-smelling flowers inside, thinking (wrongly) that would protect them from illness. Plague doctors might not be around any more, but they still visit me in my nightmares at least once a week.

TB OR NOT TB

TB is this big black rectangle that sits in the corner of your living room that you can play computer games on, and where your parents can watch boring films full of people talking and crying. No, wait a minute, that's your TV. TB is the short name for tuberculosis, which is a bacterial infection that makes you cough up blood, have terrible fevers and sweats, and lose loads of weight. Oh, and unless you get antibiotics (which didn't exist for thousands of years), then it generally makes you die. Eek.

There are signs of TB in some of the oldest people archaeologists have discovered, such as prehistoric skeletons, Ancient Egyptian mummies and my Great Aunt Prunella.

Is this meant to be some kind of joke? Because it's not funny. In fact, none of your jokes are. Prunella

Old Hippoface wrote that it was the most common disease back in Ancient Greece, where he called it 'phthisis' – maybe he was trying to spit out a fly when someone asked him to name it? He thought it was passed down through families and there was nothing you could do about it, so just shrugged his shoulders if someone turned up in his clinic with it.

Later on, it became known as 'the white plague' because it made you turn really pale (with a splash of red, when your blood decided to escape from your mouth and go all over your cardigan) and other people called it 'consumption' because it made you go so thin that it was like your body was being **CONSUMED** by the disease.

TB was a huge problem all through Sparkle Time – it killed large numbers of people and no one had the faintest idea how it was spreading. It seems so obvious now, but I guess it's like watching a quiz show on TV – we all sit there, shouting out the answers from the comfort of our sofas (well, for the easy questions anyway), but it's much harder if you're a contestant in the studio with an audience watching you. And, because no one knew how TB was infecting people, there wasn't much doctors could do to stop it.

But there's always some know-it-all adult with a terrible idea about what to do. King Charles II thought that being king gave him magical powers and that he could cure someone simply by touching them. People queued up for miles round the palace to get some of his incredible kingly wizardry – but obviously it did absolutely nothing.

1590

The microscope was invented by a man called Mike Roscope. OK, not really. In fact, no one actually knows for sure who invented it. Some people think that a man called Zacharias Janssen, whose job was making glasses, was playing around with his lenses and was suddenly like, 'Whoa, everything looks huge!' and then – *BOOM!* – one microscope. Other people think that a famous astronomer called Galileo was fiddling with his telescope and could suddenly see an insect's legs really clearly – maybe he just looked through the wrong end. Either way, someone was being silly at work, and accidentally changed science forever.

IT'S THE *JAB*SOLUTELY AMAZING INJECTION SECTION

Right, enough death and disease – it's time for some good news. In the 1700s, a disease called smallpox was sweeping through Europe, killing hundreds of millions of people – and those who survived would get really badly scarred. A doctor called Edward Jenner noticed that people who milked cows never seemed to catch smallpox, and decided to investigate why.

> Is this the good news?
Doesn't sound like it. Prunella

His theory was that they caught a much less serious disease from the cows called cow pox, and this somehow protected them from getting smallpox.

There were loads of different types of poxes: chicken pox, monkey pox, rabbit pox, sheep pox, horse pox and mouse pox. Sadly, there wasn't fox pox, which is a shame because it would have been an extremely good name for an illness.

1721

Back in the awful days when black people were enslaved, a man called Onesimus was forced to work for a rich American called Cotton Mather, who lived in Boston. Onesimus explained to Mather that in Africa they used to prevent outbreaks of smallpox by injecting children with tiny doses of it. When smallpox swept through America in 1721, Mather told the city's doctors about Onesimus' idea, and it saved loads of lives. Onesimus never got credit for his idea during his lifetime, so the very least we can do is remember the brilliant work he did.

In 1796, Edward Jenner (I don't know if he was related to Kylie and Caitlyn Jenner, but let's just imagine he was) squeezed some pus from a blister on a milkmaid who had cow pox and injected it into his gardener's eight-year-old son, James. He then injected James with actual smallpox and . . . James didn't get sick! (That's the good news.) James had received a vaccine: an injection of something harmless that stops you getting a serious illness. Vaccines have saved literally hundreds of millions of lives since then, and the best thing of all is that they're made in a lab these days, instead of from disgusting blister-pus.

HARDER, BETTER, PASTEUR, STRONGER

Right, we're pages and pages into the chapter on infections and we've whizzed through thousands of years, but scientists still hadn't worked out what actually caused them. Here are just a few of their guesses:

- smelly air
- being cold
- wet feet
- lying down too much
- being angry
- staying up late (although maybe parents just made that one up to stop their children watching TV all night, or whatever they did instead of watching telly in the olden days. Looking at paintings?)

In 1856, a bloke called Louis Pasteur came along. He was a professor of chemistry who was doing some (pretty boring but apparently important) experiments on crystals. Yawn. But one day his mate, who owned a wine shop, asked Louis to investigate why his wine was going all manky. Louis took a break from his crystals and wondered if germs might be causing the disgusto-wine.

If so, he thought heating the wine up would kill off the nasties. And he was right – the wine was saved! He then realized that the germs in milk were causing people to get sick when they drank it, so he worked out a way of heating it up to make it safe. His method (which he called pasteurization – a bit boastful, Louis?) is still used today.

PROBLEM: | PASTEUR'S SOLUTION:

MANKY WINE | BOIL IT!

GROSS MILK | BOIL IT!

NEPHEW HAVING A FEW ISSUES AT SCHOOL | STOP BOILING EVERYTHING, PASTEUR!

1786

Bethlem Hospital in London employed the
excellently named Robert Roberts as a bug catcher.
For three guineas a year (that's three gold coins, not
three guinea pigs), his job was to shake out all the patients'
mattresses and sweep up the lice and weevils and beetles
that flew out. Next time you're in a bad mood because
you've got to do some boring homework or eat
mushrooms or tidy your bedroom, just be
thankful that you're not a hospital bug catcher.

GROSSPITALS

If you have to go into hospital for any reason these days,
you know you're going to be looked after really well in
totally clean surroundings – but two hundred years ago
hospitals could actually make you sicker. They were so
filthy that rich people would pay loads of money to be
treated at home underneath their own duvet to avoid
catching any nasties in hospital.

You know the bit under your bed that never gets
hoovered? The bit with mountains of dirt and grime and
snotty old tissues and the legs of dead insects? That's
what a hospital looked like on a good day. Well, until an
amazing nurse called Florence Nightingale decided to
shake things up.

FLORENCE NIGHTINGALE: FIVE FACTS AND A LIE

1. She was known as the Lady with the Lamb because of an injured baby sheep she would always carry around with her.

2. She was named after the city she was born in – Florence in Italy.

3. Her sister was also named after the city she was born in, so got the slightly more unusual name of Parthenope.

4. She was the first woman (other than the queen) to have her picture on a UK banknote.

5. She hated having her photograph taken, and there are only a couple of photographs of her in existence. (She definitely wouldn't have used Instagram.)

6. She was a major maths whizz and developed a new type of pie chart. (That's a way to show data using pictures, not a poster with loads of different pies on it, by the way.)

1. Cute as that sounds, she was actually known as the Lady with the Lamp because she would walk around the hospital at night when the other staff had gone to bed, holding a lamp and checking up on all her patients.

Florence was born in 1820 into a rich family – she described the holiday home her parents owned as 'a small house with only fifteen bedrooms'. She knew from a very young age that she wanted to help people. After she trained as a nurse, Flo went off to work in a hospital in what is now called Turkey, where British soldiers were fighting in the Crimean War.

She was shocked that nearly half of the patients in the hospital there were dying, mostly because of infection, and she was sure it was because of terrible hygiene. She arranged for a new hospital to be built that was much cleaner, and introduced extremely strict rules about

TIME TO CLEAN THIS PLACE UP!

hand-washing. And it worked! Previously, half of all the patients were dying, and suddenly only two out of a hundred were.

When she came back to England, she set up the first-ever nursing school and wrote the first-ever book about how to be a nurse. Today there are *loads* of hospitals named after her, a fleet of aeroplanes that transport sick patients, the highest honour in nursing and even an asteroid. That's all **QUITE** impressive, but if you burp and fart at the same time it's known as 'doing an Adam Kay', which I think is much better.

SPOILSPORT!

1855

Another nurse who saved
hundreds of lives in the Crimean
War was Mary Seacole. Mary was born in
Jamaica in 1805, before moving to London and
volunteering to help in the war. She was an expert
in treating infections like cholera and yellow fever,
and was famous for riding out into battlefields to help
wounded soldiers, so they could get treated as soon
as possible. She cared for so many soldiers that she
became known as Mother Seacole. (This is a
bit unfair, because when I was a doctor, my
patients never called me Daddy Adam.)

JAMES BARRY

There was a brilliant doctor in the 1800s called James Barry, who worked in the British Army as the Inspector General of Hospitals, going from country to country and improving the hygiene conditions on the wards, to stop patients dying from infections. It was only when Dr Barry died that it was discovered they were born a woman, and lived as a man partly because otherwise they wouldn't have been allowed to work as a doctor.

MARVELLOUS, MIRACULOUS MOULD

I do a lot of things by accident. There was the time I put my phone in the tumble dryer and it never worked again (but smelled lovely). And there was the time I was staying with my Great Aunt Prunella and accidentally spilled my milkshake into her piano. Or the time I left my birthday cake on a low table that Pippin could reach, and she ate the whole thing and had terrible diarrhoea for two days (and I didn't get any birthday cake – I'm still upset about that).

> That was you?! It cost me a fortune to get that cleaned out. You total dunderhead. Prunella

But it's fair to say that none of those things changed the history of the world. In 1928, a Scottish scientist called Alexander Fleming was in a bit of a rush to go off on holiday so he didn't tidy away some little dishes full of bacteria that he'd been growing for an experiment.

He came back a couple of weeks later with a suntan and a Mickey Mouse T-shirt (I'm not sure if he went to Disneyland, actually – maybe not because it hadn't been built yet) and there was some mould growing on his dishes of bacteria.

So far so boring – mould grows on stuff if you leave it out for too long. Take a look at the socks on your bedroom floor if you need any proof. But A-Flem noticed something weird. No, not about your socks – about his dishes of bacteria. There was no bacteria whatsoever growing around the mould – it was producing a substance that killed bacteria. And he named it . . . mould juice. Luckily, he soon realized that didn't sound particularly scientific or make him seem very brainy, so he came up with a new name: penicillin. This was the first-ever antibiotic, which means a drug that kills bacteria. He won a Nobel Prize for this – and fair enough really, because it has now saved hundreds of millions of lives. Just think of all the people who could have been saved throughout this chapter if antibiotics had been around to treat people with TB and the Black Death and so many other awful illnesses.

1965

If you're on holiday in Australia and going for a swim in a lake, what's the worst creature you think you could come across? A crocodile the size of a car? Wrong. A great white shark with three hundred teeth, each one as sharp as a knife? Nope. It's much smaller than either of those – it's actually five times thinner than a single hair. I'd like to introduce you to the brain-eating amoeba. It swims up your nose and it . . . well, you can probably guess the rest. The good news is infections from these amoebas are extremely rare – it was first discovered in 1965 and there have only been a few cases since then. You're more likely to win the lottery, then immediately get struck by lightning.

THE FUTURE

Prediction time now, from my robot butler, who just finished emptying the bins (unfortunately, he emptied them all onto the sofa).

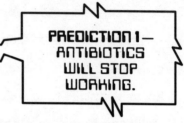

PREDICTION 1 – ANTIBIOTICS WILL STOP WORKING.

The more you use antibiotics, the less powerful they become. You know, like how if you say 'bum' once then it's a bit shocking, but if you say it all the time it isn't as effective. Or how one slice of chocolate cake is delicious, but four hundred and thirty-five slices are . . . a bit much.

Already, there are some antibiotics that have stopped being effective, and the worry is that one day all antibiotics will stop working, and it'll be just like they'd never been discovered in the first place. But don't panic: there are things we can do to stop this from happening.

First of all, antibiotics should **ONLY** be taken by people who really need them – that's for bacterial infections, not viruses or sniffles or bumsquirts. And if you're prescribed a course of antibiotics, then it's really important to take the whole lot because stopping after a few days can help bacteria become resistant to them. And, most importantly, try not to get yourself or other people ill in the first place. You can do simple things to avoid getting sick like washing your hands, blowing your nose into a tissue, and not drinking from the toilet bowl. (That last one is mainly for Pippin.)

PREDICTION 2 –
THE NEXT CHAPTER
IS MOSTLY
ABOUT POO.

I like the sound of it already.

ADAM'S ANSWERS

WHY DO WE SAY WE'RE FEELING LOUSY?

You know how sometimes your throat feels like you've been gargling drawing pins? Or your head feels like a baby hippo sat on it? Some people say when they're ill that they feel 'lousy'. They've been saying this for hundreds of years, and it used to mean that lice were literally crawling all over their body. Did you scratch yourself when you read that sentence? Me too.

WHICH NURSERY RHYME IS ABOUT THE PLAGUE?

'Baa Baa Black Death'? 'Mary Had a Little Plague'? Well, some people think it's actually 'Ring-a-ring of Roses'. Let's have a quick singalong:

Ring-a-ring of roses (A rosy-red rash that people got when they had the plague.)

A pocket full of posies (Posies were flowers that people carried around, hoping that the smell would stop any infection.)

Atishoo! Atishoo! (Sneezing from the illness.)

We all fall down! (And now it's killed you. Oops.)

Other people think it's just a silly rhyme that doesn't have anything to do with the plague, so I'll leave it to you to decide.

DID ARMIES EVER USE INFECTIONS AS WEAPONS?

They did indeed. Thousands of years ago, soldiers would dip the ends of their arrows into poo so that it was more likely that the person they shot would die from an infection. And in Sparkle Time, if they couldn't get into a city, they would sometimes catapult the body of someone who had died of plague over the walls, to kill off a bunch of people inside. (My lawyer, Nigel, has asked me to point out that it's both illegal and dangerous to catapult a plague victim's body into your enemy's back garden.)

TRUE OR POO?

RABBITS CAN TELL IF YOU'VE GOT AN INFECTION.

POO Rabbits don't know if you've got an infection, but dogs do! (Well, not all dogs. Pippin can't even tell the difference between grass and carpet, so she regularly poos on my bedroom floor.) But some very clever dogs (no offence, Pippin) have been trained to sniff out if a patient has a disease such as malaria, which is transmitted by mosquitoes. Good dog!

A DOCTOR SAVED THOUSANDS OF LIVES BY SNAPPING A HANDLE OFF A WATER PUMP.

TRUE In 1854, hundreds of people in London were dying from a disease called cholera, which caused terrible vomiting and diarrhoea. A doctor called John Snow realized that everyone who caught cholera had something in common – they got their water from one particular pump. Back in the 1800s, people didn't have taps in their houses, so if they wanted a bath, or a cup of tea, they had to go to a water pump and bring it home. John was really sure about his theory but, because germs weren't a thing that anyone knew about yet, no one really believed him. The other doctors thought that cholera was actually caused by eating 'cold fruit' like melons and cucumbers. (What?!) But John wasn't having any of it, so he snapped the handle off the water pump so no one else could get any water from it and – ta-da! – there were no more new cases of cholera. If you're ever in central London, you can visit the pump on what's now called Broadwick Street. And they still haven't put the handle back on – better safe than sorry.

SOME INFECTIONS MAKE YOU SMILE.

TRUE There's a disease called tetanus, which people get by cutting themselves on a rusty nail or being bitten by an animal. It causes muscles in your body to tighten up, and this can affect the face, causing a constant big smile – a bit like the Joker in Batman, or Pippin when she finds a huge muddy puddle to jump in. There's nothing at all funny about tetanus though: if you hurt yourself like this, it's important to be checked by a doctor, in case they need to give you a jab to stop you getting ill.

CRAZY CURES

Got a bit of Black Death? Before antibiotics, there wasn't a whole lot that could be done, but this didn't stop doctors trying. One particular favourite was to take a live chicken, pluck all the feathers out of its bottom, then press the chicken on the patient's swollen armpit. It was said to be particularly important to centre the chicken's bumhole on the middle of the armpit. Unfortunately, this didn't do anything useful whatsoever for the patient (or the chicken).

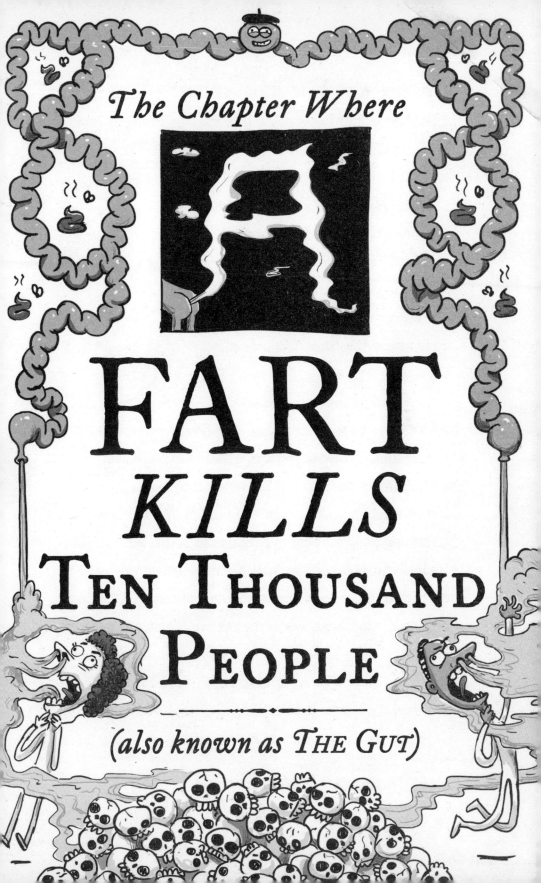

The Chapter Where **A FART** *KILLS* TEN THOUSAND PEOPLE

(also known as THE GUT)

I DON'T KNOW IF THIS COUNTS as too much information, but I'm writing this chapter from the toilet. Maybe I shouldn't have warmed up that leftover pasta for lunch after all. Anyway, I'm not the first person to have tummy trouble, and I definitely won't be the last. Humans have been obsessed with their guts ever since the first caveperson did their first cave-poo.

FINALLY, UG HAVE FRIEND.

And things have been going wrong with our insides for just as long. A few years ago, a man and a woman were on holiday in the mountains when they bumped into a man called Otzi. Otzi didn't say much to them because he'd been dead for over five thousand years, but the cold temperatures meant he had been perfectly preserved. Scientists examined him and discovered that he had worms in his intestines and ulcers in his stomach. Poor Otzi. (Not sure how they knew that was his name, by the way. Maybe he was holding his driving licence?) Anyway, I'd better get off the loo and tell you about the toilet habits of the Ancient Egyptians.

→ That's disgusting. You horrible boy. Rewrite this section when you are not on the toilet. Prunella

ANCIENT EGYPT

They may not have known that much about the body, but even the Ancient Egyptians knew that poo came out of their bums. (Although it must have been a bit of a surprise for the first person that it ever happened to. They probably screamed, *'Aaaagh!* What's going on?! Why is this brown stinky snake squirting out of my body! Call an ambulance!')

They definitely realized the guts were important because, when someone was mummified, their guts were popped into a special jar for a safe journey to the afterlife. They even had a special god who protected the guts on this journey, called Qebehsenuef. I bet Qebehsenuef was annoyed that all the other gods had cool things like the heart and the lungs to look after, and he just got a pot of pooey intestines.

The Ancient Egyptians didn't **QUITE** understand what happened to food when it went into your body to be digested though. For a start, they thought that food travelled to your heart through a series of tubes, then went down to your bumhole. (Or anus, if you want me to use proper doctory words. Which would be fair enough because I'm a trained doctor.) It seems the pharaohs and their friends got the heart and the stomach mixed up there. They reckoned the best way to treat stomach ache was by wearing a special kind of necklace, with words of encouragement written on it. I can confirm that wearing a necklace does not cure tummy ache, in case you somehow thought writing YOU CAN DO IT! on your great aunt's pearls might sort out your diarrhoea.

> Don't you dare lay your grubby hands on my jewellery. Prunella

1926

An archaeologist was having a snoop around the pyramids in Giza and found the grave of an important doctor called Iry from Ancient Egypt. His title was 'Guardian of the king's anus'. Never, ever complain again about being asked to tidy your room or clean your shoes – because this guy had it so much worse. From 9 a.m. to 5 p.m., five days a week, for his entire career, he looked after a single bumhole.

They did get some stuff right though. For example, they invented toothpaste! It didn't have nice stripes in it, and it probably tasted disgusting because it was made of crushed-up bits of rock, salt, pepper and mint, but at least they tried. And if you had toothache? Well, they treated it by sticking a dead mouse in your mouth. I'd stick to taking Calpol and lying in bed reading comics, personally.

ANCIENT GREECE

You know how, if you ever vomit up your food, it's become a horrific soup, like a blended version of your breakfast? We now understand that's because acid in the stomach has melted it, but the Ancient Greeks thought that the stomach cooked it. Kind of like a mini-oven installed inside your abdomen.

They also thought that emotions came from the gut – maybe they noticed that if they were really worried about something then they got bumsquirts and assumed it must be their gut that was getting worried. It's why we still say we have 'a gut feeling' about things, or we 'feel gutted' if something goes wrong. Once again, those Greeks were giving random parts of the body credit for stuff that the brain does. Poor brain.

I thought this was meant to be a serious textbook. Please use sensible words like 'diarrhoea' not vulgarities like 'bumsquirts'. Honestly. Prunella

The Ancient Greeks were among the first people to do bum surgery. They were particularly interested in a condition called haemorrhoids, also known as piles, which are little balls of muscle and blood vessels that look like grapes (sorry if you're eating grapes) and poke out of the bumhole, making things very sore down there. Old Hippoface, Hippocrates, came up with an operation to get rid of them. He would heat up a metal rod in a furnace until it was white-hot, then stick it on the haemorrhoids until they burned off. It worked, but I suppose you would have to decide whether it was better to have haemorrhoids or to be screaming in agony, while your bumhole sizzled like a sausage.

ANCIENT ROME

As you'll remember from the chapter on circulation (unless you've got a hole in your brain), Galen had this incredible (and incredibly wrong) theory that all the blood in your body came straight from food. According to Galen, you ate food, it went into some kind of magic turning-food-into-blood device and then . . . *ping!* Lots of lovely new blood. Hmm, not exactly how it works though, is it?

He also wrote quite a lot in his books about farting. Who can blame him? So do I! But unlike me (hopefully, otherwise you'll fail all your exams) Galen got it all totally wrong. For example, he thought that you cured farting by reading out loud, which is a big load of farty nonsense.

. . . THEN STIR ALL THE BEANS IN A BIG POT, AND ADD SOME MORE BEANS AND . . .

1000 BEAN RECIPES

SPARKLE TIME

In Sparkle Time (or the Middle Ages, if you insist on using its terrible former name for some reason), they still thought the stomach was some kind of weird internal microwave.

But they did notice that the more stuff you shoved into your mouth, the bigger you would become. One day, King William I, also known as William the Conqueror, also known as Wee Willie Conk (well, he's only known as that to me), realized that he couldn't fit on his horse any more. To the relief of his horse, he asked his doctor how to lose a bit of weight. The doctor suggested that he should probably stop eating so much.

'Perfect,' said Wee Willie Conk. 'I'll just lie in bed all day and not eat anything at all. In fact, I'll just drink wine constantly.' His doctor was probably worried by this plan, but it's a bit difficult to tell the king what to do, if you like your head still attached to your body, so he couldn't really say anything much. (My lawyer, Nigel, has asked me to point out that you shouldn't lie in bed all day and you **DEFINITELY** shouldn't drink wine all day.) Anyway, this weird diet somehow worked, and soon Willie was able to ride his horse again. It turns out he shouldn't have bothered because one morning he fell off his horse, his intestines exploded and he died. Whoops.

Fast-forward a hundred years and the king's a bloke called Henry. You might think of kings as boring people who just wear crowns and sign things with quills, but Henry was . . . How do I put this? Henry was . . . extremely interested in farting. He even employed a full-time jester called Roland the Farter. No prizes for guessing what Roland the Farter's party trick was. Yep, exactly. And Henry rewarded him for his excellent bum-work by giving him an enormous manor house and huge amounts of land. (If getting paid for farting was still a thing, Pippin would be the richest dog in the entire world.)

This is the worst book I've ever read. I recommend you delete it all and write about nice things instead, such as walks along the river and flower arranging. Prunella

GUFF TOWERS

1666

The Great Plague was sweeping through London, killing thousands of people, but doctors didn't understand about infections yet so they thought it was because of some kind of evil mist spreading through the air. And how did they suggest that people stayed plague-free? Well, everyone was advised to fart in a jar and, if anyone nearby caught the plague, then they should open the jar. They thought the bum-gas would basically beat up the plague-gas and everything would be OK. It's hard to count the number of things they got wrong with this idea, but I'm going with eight million.

BUMS AND BUZZARDS

It's now 1780 and not much has been discovered about your poo-making machinery for hundreds and hundreds of years. Luckily, an Italian whizz-kid called Lazzaro Spallanzani was about to shake things up. Spallanzani realized the stomach wasn't a weird oven or one of those big pepper grinders in Italian restaurants, but actually worked by squirting acid onto food, and that's what dissolved it! He called stomach acid 'gastric juice', which sounds a lot more delicious than it actually is.

SPALLANZANI: FIVE FACTS AND A LIE

1. As well as being a scientist, Spallanzani was also a priest and the boss of a museum.

2. He discovered that bats fly around using their ears to work out where they're going rather than their eyes. He took his pet owl (who even has a pet owl?! The olden days were crazy) and a few bats and made them fly round an obstacle course in the pitch-dark. The owl was useless, and the bats thought it was the easiest thing in the world.

3. The word zany, meaning 'crazy', comes from Spallan**ZANI** because everyone thought his ideas were so weird.

4. The first scientific paper he wrote was all about skimming stones: when you throw a rock onto the water and it bounces a few times before sploshing underwater. Luckily, he got bored with researching stones and moved on to humans.

5. Before Spallanzani, people believed that tiny insects could appear out of nowhere, from dust, which was known as spontaneous generation. Spallanzani said, 'Spontaneous poo, more like,' and proved it was a load of old twaddle.

6. He played a trick on another professor by glueing two halves of different animals together and leaving it in his office. The professor thought he'd discovered an incredible new species and published a paper about it – and then Spallanzani revealed it was all a joke. (Pranks were a bit rubbish in those days.)

3. Zany is nothing to do with Spallanzani, but actually comes from a different Italian word – 'Zanni' was a type of clown who wore a mask. Sounds more terrifying than crazy to me . . .

In case people weren't convinced by Spallanzani's theory about gastric juice, a French scientist called René de Réaumur did an experiment to prove it using his pet buzzard. Seriously, why did everyone have such weird pets? What's wrong with having a dog? (Well, I suppose my one vomits everywhere, then licks it straight back up.)

René didn't write down what the buzzard was called, so I'll assume she was called Buzzé. René fed Buzzé a diet of sponges on a string for breakfast, lunch and supper. After the sponge had been down in Buzzé's stomach for a while, René would pull on the string, and the sponge would come back out of Buzzé's beak, full of juice. And how did he prove that this stinky stomach liquid digested food? Well, he squeezed it onto a lump of raw meat and watched the meat dissolve away. Everyone in France was so impressed with his experiment that they named a station in Paris after him. (Sadly, nothing got named after poor Buzzé, even though she did all the hard work. Oh, unless she was actually called Eiffel . . .)

1822
You might have noticed
that quite a lot of important
discoveries in medicine happened
because someone got a horrible injury.
Well, here we go again – Alexis St Martin was
minding his own business one day when he got
shot in the stomach: how rude! Miraculously, he
survived, but the wound didn't heal very well,
to say the least: he was left with a massive
hole going from the outside world to the
middle of his stomach. If he ate a biscuit and
leaned forward, it would go down into his
stomach, then fall out onto the floor –
what a waste of a Jammie Dodger!

Fascinated by this hole in Alexis's tummy, a doctor called
William Beaumont hired Alexis to be his servant – for
duties including chopping wood, carrying the shopping
and . . . having hideous experiments performed on him.
Beaumont carried out over two hundred experiments on
Alexis, one of which involved Dr Beaumont licking the
inside of his stomach. Excuse me for a second while I'm
sick. OK, I'm back now. Anyway, the main benefit from
all this disgustingness is that Dr Beaumont made lots of
important discoveries, including that the stomach
produces more acid when there's food inside it.

IMPORTANT – please do **NOT** read this section out at mealtimes. In 1887, a man appeared onstage in France called Le Pétomane, which means the Fartmaniac. He could do a lot of incredible bum-based tricks, such as squirting a jet of water out of his bumhole and into the audience, farting the tune of the French national anthem, blowing out a candle with his farts, and singing 'Old Macdonald had a Farm' (with special farts for all the animal sounds).

ALL GOOD THINGS MUST COME TO AN ENDOSCOPE

These days, if a doctor is worried about a patient's stomach or intestines, they might use something called an endoscope to look inside. It's basically a tiny camera on the end of a thin, bendy tube that allows them to see your innards on a screen, like a particularly boring TV show. Before clever technology like video cameras and fibre-optic cables came along, doctors could only use straight tubes because it's impossible to see round corners. (Unless you're an alien. You're not, are you?) Unfortunately, this meant there was no way they could look down into someone's stomach because the throat and oesophagus are so bendy.

In 1868, a German doctor called Adolph Kussmaul was having a lovely night out at the theatre, watching a sword swallower, when he suddenly thought: *I know! I'll ask the sword swallower how he does this, and then I can build an endoscope that looks into the stomach!* All the other people at the theatre probably looked at him and said, 'Shh! We're trying to watch the show here!'

By then, doctors had pretty much sussed out how our guts work and the textbooks weren't too different from the ones today – although they were a lot more boring. I looked at one that had 227 pages about haemorrhoids, those bum-grapes I told you about before.

Sounds a lot better than this book. Prunella

2014

Ninety cows were hanging out in a shed in Germany, farting away happily, when the amount of fart gas in the air got so high that . . . *BOOM!* The entire place exploded. We already knew that farts were flammable, but this is the first time they'd blown up a building.

SOME WORDS ABOUT TURDS

I couldn't write a whole chapter on the gut and not have a section on poo. If I did, I'm pretty sure you'd ask for a refund, and who could blame you? Poo obviously hasn't changed much over the years – still brown, still smelly – although what we do with it has changed **A LOT**. These days, we flush it away, but in the past they used poo as medicine . . . In Ancient Egypt, your doctor would prescribe it for pretty much anything. Headache? Eat some poo. Rash? Smear some poo on it. Struggling to get pregnant? Eat some more poo. I just hope these doctors also prescribed breath mints for afterwards.

At least poo isn't involved in medicine today. Phew! Oh no, hang on – it is. There's a type of infection in the intestines that antibiotics can't always treat, and doctors realized that if they put a small pellet of poo from a healthy person into the intestines of the ill person, then it can get rid of the infection. This is called 'faecal transplantation' because if it was called 'prescribing poo' then doctors might burst out laughing in front of their patients.

THE FUTURE

Now let's hear what my robot butler has to say about the future. He's just changed my bed – unfortunately, he changed it into a wheelbarrow.

PREDICTION 1 – THERE WILL BE SURGEONS YOU CAN SWALLOW.

Until very recently, if a doctor wanted to look inside your intestines, they'd need to stick a tube inside and do an endoscopy. Obviously this wasn't particularly fun for the patient, so scientists came up with the idea of a tiny tablet that you swallow. It swims around in your innards like it's at a water park, taking hundreds of photographs, until you eventually poo it out. Much easier and much more comfortable – you just have to remember not to flush it away. In a hundred years, scientists will have worked out a way for these tiny capsules to perform actual operations, so doctors can do surgery on your intestines, and all you'll have to do is swallow a miniature remote-controlled robot.

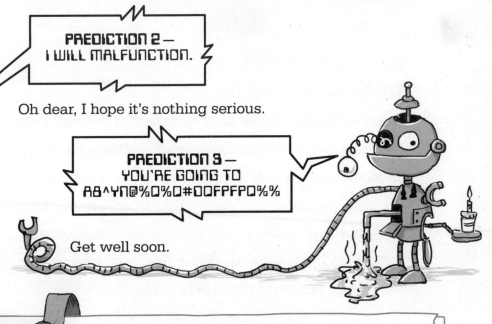

PREDICTION 2 –
I WILL MALFUNCTION.

Oh dear, I hope it's nothing serious.

PREDICTION 3 –
YOU'RE GOING TO
A8^Yⁿ@%0%0#00FPFP0%%

Get well soon.

ADAM'S ANSWERS

HOW DID DOCTORS USE TO SEW UP INTESTINES?

The first records we have of doctors sewing up people's guts are in books from India about three thousand years ago. Did they use cotton thread? Bronze wire, maybe? Or did they get giant ants, make them clamp their jaws over the wound, then twist off their bodies, leaving a line of decapitated ant heads along the wound? Yep – you guessed it! They'd basically invented a kind of staple made from ants. Surgeons still use staples to stitch intestines today (although these days no ants get decapitated in the process).

HOW DID A FART KILL TEN THOUSAND PEOPLE?

And you thought **YOUR** farts were bad – the worst they do is make everyone hold their nose and leave the room. (And maybe the odd bit of vomiting.) In Jerusalem, a couple of thousand years ago, a Roman soldier killed ten thousand people with a single fart. No, they weren't suffocated by its toxic stench – baked beans weren't on sale yet. It happened because he pulled down his pants and let out a huge fart at a crowd of people, who were so insulted they started an enormous riot and loads of people got injured. I guess the moral of this story is: think before you fart.

WHAT'S THE GREAT STINK?

It's what doctors call your bum. It was also the name for a couple of months in 1858 when there was so much poo dumped into the River Thames that London became unbelievably stinky and lots of people got ill because of all the nasties in the water supply. It led to a new system of sewers being built to stop poo from getting into people's drinking water.

WHY DID THE ANCIENT ROMANS EAT LYING DOWN?

You might have seen pictures of emperors lounging about on massive sofas, while servants dropped grapes into their mouths. Well, it was basically because they were lazy and bossy, and wanted to show off that they were far too important to do things like shove food into their own gobs. Medically, there aren't any real benefits to it, so I'm afraid you can't demand dinner in bed every day and say it's doctor's orders. In fact, eating lying down isn't particularly good for you: it makes it more likely that acid will slosh up from your stomach into your oesophagus, which can cause a pain known as heartburn. (It shouldn't be called heartburn because it's nothing to do with your heart. Maybe oesphagusburn is too difficult to spell?)

TRUE OR POO?

SHAKESPEARE WROTE FART JOKES.

TRUE Even though he was apparently the best writer who ever existed, old Shakey was a big fan of a fart joke. At least six of his plays include lines about bum-gas. For example, in *The Comedy of Errors*, a servant called Dromio says, 'A man may break a word with you, sir, and words are but wind.' Yeah, it's not great. But if a teacher ever suggests that you read some Shakespeare, you can just say that it's much too rude for you, and you should read a more sensible, suitable book. I recommend this one.

→ I don't. Prunella

THE ANCIENT ROMANS GARGLED WITH DIARRHOEA AS A MOUTHWASH.

POO Absolute nonsense. Even the Ancient Romans wouldn't do anything as strange and disgusting as that. They used . . . Oh. Urine. It was so popular that they had to import extra urine from other countries. The strangest thing is that it actually worked. Wee contains something called ammonia, which can still be found in cleaning products today. So their teeth would have looked shiny and white as a result, even if their breath stank like . . . well, like they'd just drunk a glass of wee. (My lawyer,

Nigel, has asked me to point out that you shouldn't ever gargle with wee.)

DOCTORS IN ANCIENT GREECE WOULD TASTE YOUR VOMIT.

TRUE I'm extremely glad that I didn't work as a doctor in Ancient Greece. First of all, I don't speak Ancient Greek. And, secondly, some historians think that doctors worked out what was wrong with a patient by investigating their puke. I don't mean just looking at the colour and the texture of it, which is bad enough, but also . . . how it tasted. I would have one hundred per cent quit medical school the second they told me that was part of the job. And how did they make their patients vomit? All sorts of tricks: from drinking a jug of salt water, to eating toenail clippings. Ugh, I'm feeling sick just from writing that. Excuse me for one second. *Bleeurrrrrrgh!* That's better.

CRAZY CURES

Do you grind your teeth at night? These days your doctor might suggest you wear a mouthguard while you're under the duvet. But a couple of thousand years ago the treatment was a bit more revolting. Actually, it was a lot more revolting. Doctors would make you keep a human skull on your pillow and, a few times a night, you had to give it a kiss or maybe a nice big lick – your choice! They thought grinding your teeth was a sign that you were talking to a ghost in your sleep and maybe licking a skull would help. Absolute weirdos.

SLEEP WELL.

The Chapter Where

Your Toes Fall Off & You Wash Your Hair With Ground-Up Mice

(also known as Skin)

IT'S TIME TO HAVE A LOOK AT THE SKIN – you know, the organ you can see every morning when you look in the mirror. (If you can see your heart or your lungs or your intestines when you look in the mirror, then please call a doctor quite urgently.) And yes, the skin **IS** an organ – it's not just your body's special version of orange peel, it's an actual living part of you. In fact, it's the biggest organ in the body. Well, *on* the body. Hmm. Around the body? Whatever – it's the body's largest organ, OK? Let's have a look through history at all its best zits. Sorry, I mean best bits.

We should talk about hair too – your very own built-in bobble hat and blanket. Sometimes, when it's cold, I look at Pippin and wish I had a nice thick coat like hers. Well, I mean I do have a nice thick coat, but I bought it in a shop. We used to be totally covered in hair, back when we were cavepeople – aka *aaaaaages* ago. We actually never really lost it entirely: we've all got the same amount of hair as a chimpanzee. The only difference is that our hair is a lot thinner so you can barely see it over most of our bodies. The main exception is your uncle who looks like he's got a welcome mat underneath his shirt and a sweeping brush coming out of each ear. No one really knows why we're not quite so hairy these days, but it's just as well – otherwise we'd have to constantly comb our faces and it would cost us a fortune to go to the hairdresser's.

ANCIENT EGYPT

They might have thought the brain was a useless, weird beanbag and that you cured stomach ache by wearing a necklace, but the Ancient Egyptians were pretty clued up about the skin. They took being clean extremely seriously (you could probably learn a thing or two from them – no offence, but I can smell your socks from here) and they had regular baths, although sadly they didn't have any rubber ducks. They did come up with the first-ever deodorant though, which for some reason was made out of porridge. Maybe they thought it tasted disgusting and hid it under their armpits so their parents thought they'd eaten it?

Because of their hobby of wrapping themselves up in bandages, there are loads of people from back then who are perfectly preserved, so we know a lot about their various lumps and bumps and boils and blisters. They basically had the same skin problems that we still get today, like eczema and headlice. You probably won't faint with shock if I tell you they had slightly different ways of treating their skin issues though. (Apologies if you just fainted.)

If they cut themselves, they'd make a bandage out of . . . raw meat. (Hmm, first porridge for their pits, now beef for their bandages. I guess chemists didn't exist, so they had a quick look through their kitchen cupboard instead.)

And, if they had bad spots, they'd smear some honey on them. (See?) I've got no idea if honey helps with spots – maybe it just made a load of flies swarm around their face so no one could see their zits?

If they had pus pouring out of a wound, the Ancient Egyptians would plonk a slice of mouldy bread on it. (Did they ever actually eat food or did they just use it for first aid?) They might have been on to something with the mouldy bread idea – remember Alexander Fleming and his mouldy old penicillin? What do you reckon? I sphinx so.

↳ *Is this meant to be a joke? Absolutely awful. Please can you change your surname so no one realizes I'm related to you. Prunella*

ANCIENT GREECE

In Ancient Greece, they didn't really understand the skin – Aristotle thought that it was a result of the flesh underneath going all dry and hard, like when you leave custard out for too long. But they did realize something very important: skin needs to be protected from the sun. They attempted to do this by rubbing themselves all over with olive oil – if you're wondering whether or not this works, think about what happens when you cover potatoes in olive oil and chuck them in the oven . . . They roast.

DELICIOUS!

CRUNCH!

The Ancient Greeks also had some pretty unusual ideas about baldness. They thought men lost their hair more than women because they were hotter. Not more attractive – I mean literally hotter. Those Greek geniuses reckoned that men's bodies were some kind of furnace that sizzled away all the hair on their heads. (That theory didn't quite explain the great big carpets of hair men had on their chests . . .)

Our old friend Hippoface came up with a cure for baldness. He made a lovely paste out of cumin (yum) and radishes (yum) and nettles (less yum) and pigeon poo (*aaaaagh!*). Well, I say it was a cure – it was about as effective as when I tried to teach Pippin how to speak Spanish.

ANCIENT ROME

The Romans thought that being 'beautiful' on the outside meant being healthy on the inside. This is obviously total codswallop. First of all, whatever you look like, you're beautiful – it's nothing to do with a random list of features that some idiots have decided you should have. Secondly, the shape of your nose or the colour of your hair isn't related to your health at all! I can prove it: I get so out of breath when I run for a bus that I have to sit down for half an hour – and I'm the most handsome man in the world.

> Nonsense! You're about as handsome as my pet tarantula. Prunella

If people had any blemishes, they'd plaster on tons of make-up to hide them. Make-up was made from things like sheep's sweat, horses' urine, vinegar, eggs and onions – I'd much rather have zits than wear that. I've got no idea if this gross cure worked, but it must have made people smell like the inside of a rubbish truck. If you were really rich, you might have used a kind of make-up that was very expensive, very dangerous to get hold of and just as smelly. Yep, you'd dab your face with some delightful crocodile poo.

If you wanted to get rid of wrinkles, you might treat yourself to a bath full of . . . nope, not bubbles; nope, not rose petals . . . asses' milk. Don't panic – it's nothing to do with bums – it means milk from a donkey. It didn't work, and it doesn't sound particularly fun either. I'd much rather have a bath in a huge tub of hot chocolate, with extra marshmallows.

A lot of people dyed in Ancient Rome. No, that's not a spelling mistake – this book doesn't have any spelling mistaks – they dyed their hair. If you wanted lighter hair, then you'd dip it in vinegar and maybe even sprinkle it with gold dust. If you wanted your hair to look darker, then you'd slather it in a mixture of rotting leeches and red wine. Your locks would end up lovely and dark, but you'd smell like a zombie's underpants.

If someone's hair fell out in Ancient Rome, they thought it was caused by wearing heavy helmets all day, which is total drivel. Julius Caesar was really worried about losing his hair, so to make it grow back he invented a shampoo made out of horses' teeth, ground-up mice and the fat from under a bear's skin. It didn't work at all, so that treatment was abandoned very quickly (which the horses, mice and bears will be very pleased to hear).

Caesar eventually came up with a different plan: he made a kind of headband out of laurel leaves so no one could see his lack of locks – that's why, if you see a picture of him, it looks like he's just lost a wrestling match with a hedge.

161

SPARKLE TIME

If you think of Sparkle Time (or the Middle Ages if you're still using the old-fashioned term for some stupid reason), you probably imagine a whole load of stinkiness. And I don't blame you – we know that they used to fling buckets of poo and wee out of their windows onto the streets below. (My lawyer, Nigel, has asked me to mention that you should never throw buckets of poo and wee out of your window, and you should always use the toilet instead. Even if your dad is underneath the window and it would be hilarious to do it.)

But it's totally untrue that they didn't wash themselves. They actually took cleanliness extremely seriously and they didn't just bathe regularly, they believed having baths was a cure for all sorts of illnesses, including headaches and diarrhoea. (I hope their diarrhoea wasn't too bad, otherwise the bath water would have turned brown quite quickly.)

1513

Since the beginning of time, people have been trying to make their skin look smooth and not like my Great Aunt Prunella's – her face is as wrinkled as a squashed sultana. For thousands of years, people have believed that there's a Fountain of Youth somewhere in the world, which makes you look instantly young again if you drink from it, and in 1513 a Spanish explorer called Juan Ponce de León set sail to look for it. He never found it (well, unless there's a very young-looking 500-year-old wandering around) but he did become the first European to set foot in Florida. So we lost out on eternal youth, but we got Disney World instead. Which would you prefer?

I've never been so insulted in my life. You are in big trouble, young man. Prunella

Not everyone in Sparkle Time was quite so clean though. Queen Isabella of Spain once boasted that she'd only had two baths in her entire life! She must have stunk like a turnip in a sewer – but of course no one will have told her that, in case they ended up with their head disconnected from their body. . . And, talking of heads, whether you lived in a palace or on a park bench, the chances are you were covered in headlice. They didn't call them lice though – they were known as 'worms with feet', which sounds far more disgusting (and is biologically very inaccurate). We know now that you catch headlice because they jump from one person's hair to another's when they're really close, like when a hero in an action movie jumps from roof to roof. In Sparkle Time, they thought that lice just magically appeared, as if they'd been teleported on to your head from the planet Louse.

Unfortunately, there's more to lice than an itchy head and a special comb – there are other, much more disgusting members of the louse family. (Much like there are much more disgusting members of my own family

→ Excuse me?! Prunella

than me.) There's another type of louse called the body louse or, to use its Latin name, *Pediculus humanus humanus*. (Nope, I've no idea why it has the same name twice. That's like if I was called Adam Kay Kay.) Headlice don't carry diseases, but the body louse does – and back then they were having a massive party.

→ Adam Idiot Idiot, more like. Prunella

INVITATION

Venue: Skin
Date: Sparkle Time
Time: Constantly
Theme: Disgusting
Menu: You

When the body louse chomps down on a person, it can cause a disease called typhus. Typhus is very rare these days because it can be treated with antibiotics, but in Sparkle Time it was a particularly grim illness. Typhus starts with a terrible headache and a really high fever, and then a rash that covers the whole body. And that's only the beginning! Next, the person's face swells up, and they start behaving really strangely, doing things like running around naked and screaming. Sounds awful, right?

Well, stay with me: we're only halfway through. They'd then flake out and lie down all the time, before their fingers and toes rotted away and they smelled like the alleyway behind the takeaway round the corner from me where no one's collected the rubbish for nearly a year. Would not recommend. (Typhus **OR** the takeaway.) And after that? What, you want more? Fine, they died.

In Sparkle Time, posh people were very keen not to get a suntan. It wasn't because they knew the sun could damage their skin or cause wrinkles so that their faces would look like a screwed-up piece of paper. And it wasn't because they knew it could lead to cancer. They didn't want a tan because people might think they got it from working outside on a farm and reckoned they were far too important to do a job like that. (These posh people sound pretty terrible.) Because sunscreen hadn't been invented, they protected their faces from the sun by using masks. But not like the masks people wear to protect themselves from things like coronavirus. These ones didn't have strings to tie round your ears – you had to bite down on it so it stayed in place.

Honestly, Pippin could have come up with a better design. How are you meant to order your lunch with a mask between your teeth? Try saying, 'One chocolate milkshake and large fries, please,' with your teeth clamped shut – it could have devastating results. They might mishear you and give you a banana milkshake (yuck). Worse still, how are you supposed to eat your lunch with a mask in your teeth?

IT'S AN ORGAN

It took until the 1500s for humans to realize that there was anything more to the skin than just a load of wrapping paper that stops our kidneys falling onto the pavement. This was all down to a man called Andreas Vesalius – he looked a bit more closely at the skin and realized it was made up of all sorts of different layers, and it had pores that let sweat out, and nerves that felt things.

ANDREAS VESALIUS: FIVE FACTS AND A LIE

1. His real surname was van Wesel, but he changed it so it sounded posher and more like Latin. (And less like he was a weasel.)

2. He was so good at university that they made him a professor of surgery on his final day as a student. What an absolute swot.

3. He discovered that women only have one uterus, not three.

4. For thousands of years, everyone used to think that men had more teeth than women until Vesalius proved this wrong . . . by counting them.

5. He discovered that nerves are solid, not hollow tubes full of weird magic.

6. Once, when he was cutting up a dead body (seriously did none of these guys ever fancy tennis as a hobby instead?), he noticed that the heart was still beating – oops, the person was still alive! And then they died from being cut open – double oops! And then he was arrested for murder – triple oops!

WHAT AM I LIKE?!

CLASSIC VESALIUS!

3. That's not true, but doctors did used to think that the uterus was divided into two different sections (for twins, maybe?). Vesalius was the person who proved that there was no wall in the middle of it.

THE TERRIBLE TRUTH ABOUT SOLDIERS' SOCKS

There's nothing fun about fighting a war – you're miles away from home, there are bombs dropping everywhere and people you've never met are trying to kill you. Not recommended. And, as if all that wasn't bad enough, in the First World War, soldiers' skin was trying to kill them too. They fought from trenches, which are basically long ditches dug into the ground: wet, muddy, horrible and even stinkier than your bedroom.

Soldiers would stay in these damp conditions for weeks at a time, never changing their socks or shoes (because trenches didn't have en-suite bathrooms and washing machines), and this would eventually cause a condition called trench foot. Their feet would get so damp that they'd swell up and literally rot. Quite often soldiers with trench foot wouldn't be able to take their boots off because their feet had swollen up so much, and if they did manage to then (sorry – this sentence is about to get disgusting) sometimes bits of their feet would stay behind in their boots.

This foot-based nightmare eventually got sorted out by forcing every single soldier to have a foot buddy who would inspect their mate's feet once a day to check them over and cover them in oil made from whale blubber. (Seriously, is there any animal that hasn't been involved in weird cures over the years?)

Some soldiers also got something called frostbite, which happens when it's really, really, really cold. Your fingers and toes go white and numb, and if they're not warmed up soon then crystals form under the skin – like a human ice lolly. In severe cases, fingers and toes even have to be amputated. (My lawyer, Nigel, has asked me to mention that these amputated fingers and toes are not actually ice lollies and should under no circumstances be eaten in the park on a sunny day.)

2001
Trench foot made an unwelcome reappearance, and this time it wasn't because of a war: it happened at the Glastonbury Festival in England. People were keeping their shoes and socks on for days and days in rainy, muddy weather and . . . their feet started to rot.

YOU DISGUSTING MONSTERS. Prunella

The moral of this story is: CHANGE YOUR SOCKS, YOU DISGUSTING MONSTERS.

WHO WANTS TO BE A MILLIONHAIR?

Hair can make you extremely rich. No, not by shaving it all off and knitting it into a range of disgusting jumpers – I mean that every year people around the world spend about 100 billion dollars on hair products. In 1905, a woman called Madam C. J. Walker set up a company making shampoos, combs and lotions designed for black women. She started with $1.05 in savings and soon became the first-ever female self-made millionaire in America. Throughout her life, Madam Walker made sure that other women had opportunities, giving jobs to thousands of women and making a rule that the head of the company she set up must always be female.

SAVE YOUR SKIN

Even though people have been covering up their skin to avoid sunburn for thousands of years, it was only about a hundred years ago that anyone realized the connection between sun damage and skin cancer. Then, in 1962, a science student called Franz Greiter got terrible sunburn when he was skiing in the mountains, and decided he needed to invent something to stop this happening again.

1915

For as long as humans have been hanging out on Earth, they've been affected by a horrible disease called leprosy. It's caused by a bug called *Mycobacterium leprae* (if you ever need its full name to write it a letter) and it attacks the nerves, so people with leprosy can't feel any pain. Not feeling pain doesn't make you a superhero; it just means that those parts of the body are more likely to get badly injured because you can't tell if you're getting burned, for example. For thousands of years, there wasn't much that could be done to help people with leprosy. But in 1915 a young African American scientist called Alice Ball invented the first-ever effective treatment – she adapted a traditional medicine called chaulmoogra oil so it could be safely injected into the body and cure patients of this awful disease. Very sadly, she died before her findings could be published and her evil boss pretended that it was all his idea – luckily, he got rumbled and we all now know that Alice was the genius.

He originally called it Glacier Cream (which sounds like a delicious dessert) but then renamed it Piz Buin, after the mountain where he first turned tomato-coloured. Franz Greiter went on to become a champion skier and a famous scientist, and he also holds the world record for eating the most cheese in ten minutes. Actually, sorry – that's not true. I've got that world record (unofficially).

THE FUTURE

I've just asked my robot butler to draw the curtains (he did a beautiful oil painting of them) and now he's going to make some predictions.

PREDICTION 1 — A MACHINE WILL SCAN YOUR SKIN FOR PROBLEMS.

Scientists have actually already invented a machine that you walk into and it looks at every single centimetre of your skin. A bit like those security scanners you step into at the airport, except for these skin ones you have to be naked. (My lawyer, Nigel, has warned me that you shouldn't walk through the security scanners at the airport without any clothes on, otherwise you'll probably get arrested and not be able to go on holiday.) These scanners will look at every boil on your bum and nodule on your nose, then give an instant diagnosis and suggest the right lotion or potion for you to take. They will even be able to tell the difference between the harmless little moles that most of us have and early signs of skin cancer, by looking at their exact shape, size and colour. And, by picking up cancer early, that means it's much easier to treat and lives can be saved.

Agh! Pippin!

WHY WOULD YOU BOIL YOUR COMB IF YOU LIVED IN 1900?

No, not to make a lovely comb soup. Scientists thought that baldness was caused by a kind of bacteria, and if you didn't boil your comb, then you might 'catch' baldness, like you'd catch a cold. To be honest, in those days, I think you could probably say any old nonsense like 'licking an eagle gives you asthma' and people would believe you.

WHICH FAMOUS QUEEN WAS KILLED BY HER MAKE-UP?

Elsa from *Frozen*. (No, not really – she's fine.) It was Queen Elizabeth I, who wore make-up made from lead that was so white that her face became the colour of printer paper. What's the problem with that? Well, lead is very poisonous and gets absorbed through the skin – and she was said to wear so much of it that it looked like she'd covered her face in a thick layer of Play-Doh. All the portraits of her make her look extremely glamorous and wrinkle-free – that could have been because of the make-up or because if she wasn't happy with her picture then the artist would be sent straight to prison. (I wish I could send people to prison if they put a picture of me that I don't like up on Instagram.)

WHY WOULD YOU PUT SOME OF YOUR HAIR IN A BOTTLE AND BURY IT IN THE GARDEN?

To prevent witches from casting spells on you, of course. Well, if you lived in the seventeenth century, that is. And if you believed in witches. Talking of which (or talking of witch), in Sparkle Time, they thought that if you had more than two nipples you probably practised the Dark Arts. It's actually extremely common to have more than two nipples. About one in twenty people do – Harry Styles has four! – and none of them fly around on a broomstick.

TRUE OR POO?

DOCTORS USED TO PUT TATTOOS ON THEIR PATIENTS.

TRUE In fact, they still do. Thousands of years ago, if a patient had a condition that left them with a mark on their eyeball, then instead of treating it docs would tattoo it to cover it up – ouch! Today tattoos are sometimes used if a patient is having radiotherapy, a form of treatment for cancer that involves firing invisible beams into them to kill off the abnormal cells. To make sure the beams are lined up in exactly the right place every time the patient comes to hospital, doctors often tattoo tiny dots onto their skin.

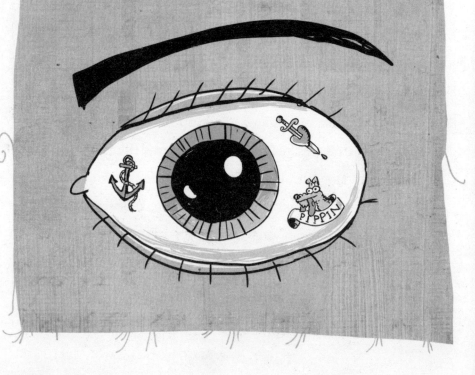

MOLES ON YOUR SKIN CAN PREDICT THE FUTURE.

POO Only robot butlers can predict the future – but in the sixteenth century they reckoned they could have a go. They thought the moles on your skin were basically a map of everything that was going to happen in your life. A spot on your neck – that was a sign you'd get suffocated at some point. Eek. A mole on your right hand meant you were about to have some good luck, and one near your belly button meant you would spend your life being lazy and greedy.

COLLECTING FINGERNAILS COULD MAKE YOU EXTREMELY RICH.

TRUE Not just any old fingernails though – in Sparkle Time, people would pay loads of money for fingernails from saints. Yes, long-dead saints. Quite how anyone knew that these were saintly fingernails and not just clippings from some local builder I have no idea. If you want to check out a set of holy fingernails, then pop over to Assisi in Italy, where St Clare's are still on display in a lovely vase.

CRAZY CURES

Mercury isn't just the name of the planet nearest to the sun. It's also a kind of metal – an extremely poisonous one. Deadly. Lethal. You'd be safer booking a two-week holiday on the planet Mercury than drinking mercury. But guess what? People have been taking it for centuries to help clear up their skin disorders. A Chinese emperor called Qin Shi Huang thought it would do more than just cure his acne – he reckoned it would make him live forever and be able to walk on water. (Saves taking a ferry, I suppose.) Unfortunately, it did the opposite of making him live forever and he died shortly afterwards. Of mercury poisoning.

The Chapter With
Clouds
of
Crud
&
400 Million
Hiccups

(also known as THE LUNGS)

I DON'T KNOW IF YOU'VE EVER TRIED BREATHING,

but I really recommend it. Oxygen whooshes into your mouth or your nose, then your lungs sneak it into the blood so your heart can whizz it off round your body to your chin and your shin and your skin. Then, finally, the lungs puff out the waste products, aka carbon dioxide, aka lung poo. (Please do **NOT** write 'lung poo' in your exams.) You know all that, obviously, because you live in the twenty-first century. But how about back in the days before they had broadband and bicycles and bums? (Actually, they always had bums. I must remember to go back and change that.)

ANCIENT EGYPT

Our pharaoh friends knew the lungs were kind of important, but they didn't have any real idea of what they did. They thought they were quite a nice shape though, so they made lots of clothing and jewellery with lungs drawn on them. They even had chairs with lungs engraved on the back. I was going to call them a bunch of weirdos, but people today wear clothes and jewellery with hearts on, which actually isn't that different, although Valentine's Day cards might not be as popular if they had a big old pair of lungs on the front.

When it came to mummification time, the Ancient Egyptians thought the lungs were less important than the heart, so they went into a jar rather than going back into the body. I don't really know why they loved the heart so much more than the other organs – it's probably just a bit like the way I'm my parents' favourite, and when it comes to my brothers and sister they say, 'Yeah, they're OK, I guess.' The lung jar had a special god to protect it called Hapy.
(Hapy sounds like he should have a massive smiley face, but I've just looked at a picture of him and he's got a baboon's head and is utterly terrifying.)

You're certainly not my favourite – I prefer your dog. And I don't particularly like your dog. Prunella

Hi! I'M HAPY!

Despite all the Ancient Egyptians' careful preparations, it turns out the organs didn't whizz off to the afterlife after all: they just stayed in their jars for thousands of years. This meant that when archaeologists cracked open the pyramids, there were loads and loads of perfectly preserved pickled innards that we've been able to have a look at. (Well, not me personally – other people did it.) When they examined the lungs, they saw something very surprising: the lungs turned into bats and flew away. OK, fine – it wasn't quite as surprising as that. They noticed that these Ancient Egyptian lungs had been damaged by pollution – the same as our lungs are today. It was probably caused by particles getting in the air from all the mining and metalwork going on, rather than factories and Ferraris, because I'm pretty sure they didn't have Ferraris in those days.

I've checked. They definitely didn't have Ferraris.

ANCIENT GREECE

If you were reading a book like this one in Ancient Greece, then the chapter on the lungs would just say, 'All the lungs do is cool down the heart.' Then you'd turn to the next chapter, safe in the knowledge that the lungs are just a pair of rib-based icebergs. For centuries, we've always just assumed that our teachers are right – maybe you should stop thinking that. I mean, these Greek guys got it pretty wrong . . .

Let's talk about strangling now. (My lawyer, Nigel, has asked me to mention that I'm not suggesting you strangle anyone.) Surely the Ancient Greeks knew that if you strangled someone and stopped the air getting into the body, then that person would end up kind of . . . dead? So that must have given them a bit of a clue about the lungs? Amazingly, no. They thought that if someone couldn't breathe, they died because their heart had become too hot.

There was only one person in Ancient Greece who thought this all sounded a bit wrong. Please welcome to the stage . . .

EMPEDOCLES!

Finally, someone to point out how weird their theories were and reveal that . . . Oh. Empedocles thought that we actually breathe through our skin. Go away, Empedocles.

EXIT

ANCIENT ROME

I'm in a good mood so I'll be generous here. The Ancient Romans spotted that the diaphragm moved up and down and that's what made the lungs expand. But that's as far as their lung discoveries went, really.

They still believed in the whole 'breathing is the heart's air-conditioning system' thing. There were two main reasons for this. Firstly, the Romans thought that if the air contained anything that the body actually needed then we wouldn't have to breathe it out. (It's lucky we don't do that, otherwise we'd puff up like massive blimps and float away.) And the second, more important reason is that they were absolute nincompoops.

NINCOMPOOPS

NINCOMPOOPER
SCOOPER

SPARKLE TIME

In Sparkle Time (ugh, fine, the Middle Ages), they didn't have any better ideas about how the lungs worked, but they started to have a go at treating patients who had difficulty breathing. They couldn't just pop into a branch of Boots, so most of their medicine came from herbs and flowers. Better than making them from manky old bread, I guess. There was a saying in Sparkle Time that went, 'How can a man die if he has sage in his garden?' Well, quite easily as it turns out because everyone from back then is dead now, however much sage was growing in their flower beds. But they were on to something: a lot of medicines we use these days come from plants – for instance, one of the most powerful painkillers in the world is made from poppies.

Unfortunately, they weren't great at working out which flowers to treat people with. They thought because God had invented diseases, God had also invented a specific treatment for every single disease, and all they had to do was find it, like some weird puzzle God had set for them as homework. They reckoned God would have made this easier for them by putting a clue on every cure, so doctors were on a constant treasure hunt, searching for roots that looked a bit like mouldy kidneys, or flowers that had the same colour as a skin rash. If someone had an infection in their lungs, they found a plant with leaves that looked like diseased lungs and made the patient scoff down loads of that. Obviously it didn't work at all – because plants don't look anything like the conditions they treat. But that particular plant is still known as lungwort, if you like facts. If you don't like facts, you can probably stop reading this book because it's a book of facts.

I wish I could, but I promised you I'd read the whole awful thing. Prunella

YOUR SPOTTY-BUM PLANT IS READY!

'TIS FOR A FRIEND . . .

LEECHES 3 FOR 2

PRESCRIPTIONS

LEONARDO DA VINCI

Leonardo da Vinci was one of the most famous artists in the history of the world ever – the *Mona Lisa*, with her famous smile, is probably the most well-known painting of all time. (It's pretty good, if you like that sort of thing, although I once did a drawing of a horse wearing trousers that was much better.) Why are we going on about art when we're in the middle of some serious breathing business? No, I haven't suddenly given up on the lungs and started writing about famous painters instead. The thing with Leo is, he wasn't just great at scribbling, he was also extremely important when it came to working out the mysteries of the human body.

Adam Kay

LEONARDO DA VINCI: FIVE FACTS AND A LIE

1. He wrote backwards, so you can only read his notes if you hold them up to a mirror. Maybe he didn't want anyone to read them? He was left-handed, so perhaps it made it less likely he'd smudge his ink? Or he could have just been showing off.

2. He was totally self-taught. (This doesn't mean that you're allowed to bunk off school and say, 'Well, da Vinci didn't need to go to lessons!')

3. He invented the helicopter. He didn't fly around Italy in a helicopter – he just designed it. No one could be bothered to actually make it for more than four hundred years.

4. He invented the parachute. (In case he fell out of his helicopter.)

5. He invented the machine gun.

6. He spent twelve years building the world's biggest-ever statue, and then just before it was completed it got totally destroyed in a war. I hate it when that happens.

5. He might have invented a lot of things, but the machine gun wasn't invented for centuries after he died. He did invent a type of crossbow that could fire loads of arrows really quickly, so maybe you should have half a mark if you thought this was true.

Leo used his excellent artistic skills (although mine are still better, never forget that) to draw the most accurate diagrams ever of the body and all its organs. In order to do this, he cut up about thirty bodies. (They were already dead – no need to phone the Italian police.) He wasn't particularly interested in anatomy; he mostly did all this chopping up of dead people because he thought it would help improve his drawing. (My lawyer, Nigel, has asked me to point out that this is a terrible idea and that you should practise your art by drawing plants or vegetables or something. It's less messy too.)

Because anatomy was a bit of a hobby for old Leo (the way that your hobby is picking your nose), he never published any of these super-detailed drawings, and most of them went completely unnoticed for hundreds of years. It's a bit of a shame really, because if he had published them we would have understood how the lungs worked about three hundred years before we did. Plus, people who lived at the same time as him would have found out about his amazing inventions and Henry VIII could have travelled everywhere by helicopter . . . Important: don't make the same mistake Leo did – if you invent something amazing, then tell everyone immediately. Especially if it's a machine that stops Pippin's farts smelling so awful.

One of da Vinci's lung-based discoveries was that it's impossible to breathe through your nose and your mouth at the same time. Try it! See? We think he proved this by trying to play two flutes at once – one through his mouth and one through his nose – and found that he couldn't do it. If his neighbours spotted him doing this experiment through the window, they must have thought he'd gone completely bananas. (Then again, they saw him cutting up loads of dead bodies and never said anything.)

WILLIAM HARVEY

So, with Leo's notebooks all hidden away in his drawer, maybe in the seventeenth century William Harvey would be the bloke to figure out what the lungs did? After all, he was the brainbox who worked out circulation. Unfortunately not. Turns out he was like a pop star who only has one good tune and then everything afterwards sounds like a cat vomiting.

He thought the lungs made the body float upwards and that's why we stood upright – maybe he got them confused with helium balloons? Noticing that dogs and cats have got smaller lungs than humans, he reckoned that's why they have to wander around on four legs instead of two. *Okaaaaaaay*. He wasn't a **TOTAL** lung-loser though. He did work out that exercising is good for your lungs, so we can thank him for that. (Or blame him, if you hate PE.)

MICE TO SEE YOU

It wasn't until a hundred years later, in 1774, that a bloke called Joseph Priestley came along and helped everyone work out what was actually happening in those spongey old lungbags. He had a theory that the air we breathe wasn't just one single gas, but it was actually lots of different gases mixed together, and one of them was a particularly important one called oxygen. (He didn't call it oxygen though. He gave it the slightly less snappy name of 'dephlogisticated air'.)

Joey worked out how important oxygen is by doing experiments on mice. Look away now if you have a pet mouse, or if you really, really love mice, or if you are a mouse. He realized that if he put a mouse in a jar, it would eventually die because all the oxygen would run out.

But if he put a mouse in a jar that also had a mint plant in it, the mouse didn't die because the plant was puffing out oxygen, which meant the mouse always had plenty of it to breathe. After he'd done this experiment, he held a quick mouse funeral, and told the world about this amazing new gas.

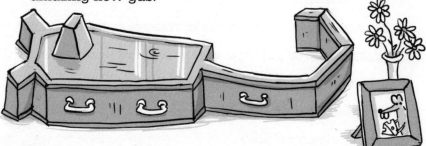

He tried breathing in pure oxygen himself and found that it made him more alert, more energetic and much better at dancing. (I might have invented the bit about dancing, if I'm totally honest.)

1922

A man called Charles Osborne hiccupped. So what's the big deal? He was weighing a pig while it happened. Still not impressed? OK, well, he hiccupped every couple of seconds and didn't stop for the next sixty-eight years. After about 400 million hiccups, one day he suddenly stopped! Hooray! And then the next year he died. Oh dear.

SMOKING IS CHOKING AND I'M NOT EVEN JOKING

I don't smoke, and you probably shouldn't either – it makes you smell like a bin that's on fire and gives you yellow teeth and brown nails, plus it literally destroys your lungs and knackers tons of other organs too. And you spend your life shivering outside doorways with a burning tube in your hand and ash all over your clothes. Seven million people die from smoking every year – that's more than the population of entire countries, like Denmark or New Zealand! And did I mention that it stinks worse than almost any fart you will ever smell? Even Pippin's. ⟶

I know full well that you blame a lot of your own intestinal gas on your dog, and I think you should tell your readers this. Prunella

There's nothing new about smoking – people were doing it in America about five thousand years ago. I can forgive them for smoking in those days because nobody realized how dangerous it was. Tobacco (which is the smelly stuff inside cigarettes) eventually made its way to the UK around five hundred years ago. King James I wasn't particularly impressed by smoking – he didn't know it was bad for your health, but he did realize it made everyone smell like a dead pigeon, so he increased the tax on it by over four thousand per cent. That's like if you went into the shop to buy your favourite chocolate bar (I'll have a KitKat, thanks) and it cost £30. Would you still buy it? Yeah, me too.

His plan didn't make smoking go away. It actually got more and more popular as the years went on. In the 1940s, eight out of ten British men smoked, and four out of ten women. All the most famous sports stars and Hollywood actors smoked and people thought it was a really glamorous thing to do. Doctors would even appear on adverts saying things like, 'This brand doesn't make your throat as sore!' It's a bit like doctors recommending cutting your ear off with a rusty knife rather than having it bitten off by a shark – neither of them are a particularly good idea.

In 1929, a German doctor called Fritz Lickint did a study that showed smoking causes lung cancer, but everyone totally ignored him. This was partly because most doctors smoked and they didn't want to even consider that it could be true. Or maybe they didn't read Fritz's article because they were outside smoking at the time. It took another twenty years for people to take the dangers of smoking seriously, and even longer to stop it being advertised and for smoking indoors to be banned. And yet there are still nearly a billion smokers in the world. Stub it out!

BAD AIR DAY

Pollution has been around ever since humans started barbecuing sabre-toothed-tiger sausages outside their caves. Any time you burn something, it releases substances into the air, and some of those – spoiler alert – aren't so great for your lungs.

Things got quite a bit worse when factories started springing up, spewing out all sorts of hideous chemicals. And then cars began to replace horses – the only toxic emissions our four-legged friends made were brown and had to be shovelled off the ground. Plus, before radiators were a thing, houses used to be kept warm by burning coal, which would send up great big clouds of crud into the sky.

In the 1950s, London was famous around the world, not for the Beefeaters or Big Ben or my Great Aunt Prunella's awful cooking, but for the terrible quality of the air.

I hope you're not referring to my turnip stew. It's a family delicacy. Delete that sentence immediately. Prunella

This air was so polluted you could literally see it. I know, right? It was known as a 'pea soup' fog because the air looked like . . . thick pea soup. It didn't smell like pea soup though. It was so full of poisons that the whole of London stank of rotten eggs – it basically smelled as if everyone who lived there had spent twelve years eating only baked beans. It seeped into people's houses under cracks in their doors and gaps in their walls, so you couldn't even escape the coughing by staying inside. If you did wander outside, you'd come back covered in soot, like you'd just climbed down a chimney. Or you'd get home with your wallet missing because thieves were able to steal things from you, and you wouldn't be able to see which direction they'd run away.

But worst of all was the damage it did to people's health. Over four thousand people died in just a couple of days because of this terrible pollution, and thousands more died afterwards. There were so many deaths that undertakers ran out of coffins and florists ran out of flowers for funerals. Luckily, we've learned lessons from tragedies like this, and now governments everywhere are trying to cut down on emissions, not just to protect the planet, but to protect all our lungs too.

ASTHMA

You've heard of asthma – the wheezy diseasey (a poem! For free!) – which people keep under control by using inhalers and other medicines. I'm pretty sure you know someone who has it because it affects one in twelve people. If you don't know anyone who has it, maybe you've only ever met ten people.

But it's not a modern disease like coronavirus or bum pox (which is so modern that I've only just invented it). Asthma has been around for a really long time. There are books from China and Egypt thousands of years ago which talk about it. The first treatment we know about for asthma was from Ancient Greece, where it was prescribed by a doctor called Aretaeus of Cappadocia. Imagine being so famous that people knew you just by your first name and the place you're from! I'd be Adam of Oxfordshire, my dog would be Pippin of the Manky Old Dog Bed that Smells of Sick. Anyway, Aretaeus of Cappadocia might have been very famous, but he wasn't very good at treating asthma. His prescription was owl's blood mixed with wine. Delicious, but not very effective.

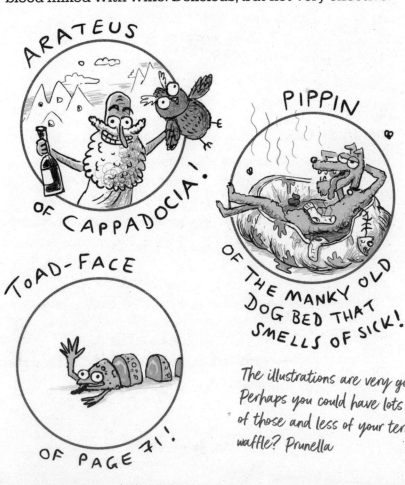

ARATEUS OF CAPPADOCIA!

PIPPIN OF THE MANKY OLD DOG BED THAT SMELLS OF SICK!

TOAD-FACE OF PAGE 71!

The illustrations are very good. Perhaps you could have lots more of those and less of your terrible waffle? Prunella

You might think that asthma cures couldn't get any worse than that. Nope! Poor asthmatics over the years have been subjected to having cold water poured over their heads, smoking (which would make it much worse) and eating honey (yum!) mixed with millipedes (yuck!). Some doctors even prescribed the very poisonous arsenic in the 1800s, which definitely stopped people wheezing – mainly because they were dead. Suddenly an occasional suck on an inhaler doesn't sound quite so bad, does it?

2015

A woman in Australia started coughing up blood and struggling to breathe so she was rushed to the nearest hospital (which is a very sensible thing to do if you're coughing up blood and struggling to breathe). The doctors did an X-ray of her lungs and saw there was a lump of metal in there. They asked her if she'd been breathing in any metal recently and she said, 'Umm . . . no?' so they did an operation to see what was going on. They removed the object and found it was one of her earrings. It turns out that she'd pulled her asthma inhaler out of her handbag one day and an earring had fallen into the end of it. She took a puff and . . . whoosh . . . her earring was a bit more inside the lung than it should have been. And that's why inhalers come with a cap to put over the end.

THE FUTURE

And now some predictions from my robot butler. He's spent all morning planting bulbs in the garden (and now none of my lights work).

**PREDICTION 1 —
YOUR INHALER WILL BE
REALLY SMART.**

No, I'm afraid it won't be able to do your maths homework for you or help you cheat in exams, but it will have sensors on it that detect if you're near a certain type of pollen or a load of pollution that might give you an asthma attack, so you can go somewhere else. Or it'll tell you if there's loads of dust in your bedroom, so you can clean it all up. (Yeah, sorry about that.) These ingenious inhalers can also let your doctor know how much you're using them, in case they need to increase the dose.

**PREDICTION 2 — PIPPIN
WILL POO IN YOUR OTHER SHOE.**

Ugh. I've only just finished cleaning the first one.

2018

A Croatian man called Budimir Šobat
broke the world record by holding his breath
underwater for 24 minutes and 11 seconds. Well,
they say he's a man, but I hope they checked that he
wasn't actually a dolphin wearing swimming trunks. Most
people can only hold their breath for something like a
minute at the most. (My lawyer, Nigel, has asked me to
point out that under no circumstances should you try
to beat Budimir's record.)

ADAM'S ANSWERS

IS IT POSSIBLE TO HAVE A LUNG TRANSPLANT?

It's very possible, yes, which is excellent news for over
three thousand patients every year whose lungs stop
working properly and need a spare. The first successful
lung transplant took place in 1981, and was actually a
heart–lung transplant, which means both lungs and the
heart were replaced at the same time. It wasn't until a
few years later that doctors first performed a lung
transplant on its own. (Maybe they couldn't work out
how to unscrew the lungs from the heart?)

WHY DO PEOPLE SAY 'BLESS YOU!' WHEN YOU SNEEZE?

In ancient times, people thought a sneeze meant evil spirits were trying to get into you, so they'd ask God to bless them to make the spirits think twice about their invasion. In Germany, they say '*Gesundheit!*'; in France, they say '*A vos souhaits!*'; and I say 'Oi! You've got snot all over me!' I don't understand why people say 'Bless you!' when you sneeze but not when you burp or fart – it doesn't make any sense.

ACHOO!

WHAT IS AN IRON LUNG?

No, it's not a kind of lung transplant made from melted-down radiators. There's a very serious disease called polio, which can stop the muscles we need for breathing from working. Luckily, polio has almost completely disappeared from the world because of clever old vaccines but it used to affect hundreds of thousands of people. These days, if someone can't use their breathing muscles for any reason, doctors can put a tube into their mouth connected to a machine that inflates their lungs. But before this was invented patients had to go into an iron lung.

It was like a big metal filing cabinet that you would slide inside with your head sticking out of one end and your feet out of the other. The pressure inside the iron lung would go up and down and up and down, which puffed the chest in and out and in and out, and allowed the patient to breathe, but it made it very difficult for them to have a swim or play the cello.

TRUE OR POO?

DOCTORS USED TO THINK THAT PARROTS COULD STOP YOU GETTING CHEST INFECTIONS.

TRUE Before they understood about infections, doctors thought that people got illnesses in their lungs because the air was too 'stiff'. (Stiff? What were they even talking about?) They reckoned the best way to cure 'stiff' air was to make loud noises, such as banging drums, firing guns and letting parrots squawk around. Not only was this totally useless, but there's actually a lung infection that you can catch from parrots. (It's called psittacosis if you like knowing things that your teachers don't.)

UH OH.

ALEXANDER THE GREAT INVENTED AN OPERATION THAT IS STILL USED TODAY.

TRUE One day Alexander the Great was having dinner with some of his soldiery mates. Suddenly one of them turned blue and collapsed to the ground – he'd got a chicken bone stuck in his windpipe and wasn't able to breathe. Alex had a clever plan: he got out his sword and cut a hole in the soldier's neck, so air could flow into his lungs. This is a procedure that's sometimes performed by doctors, called a tracheotomy. (My lawyer, Nigel, has asked me to point out that if someone is choking on their food then the correct thing to do is to push upwards on their ribs from behind, using something called the Heimlich manoeuvre, not to stick a sword in their neck.)

SMOKING USED TO BE ALLOWED AT SCHOOL.

TRUE During the Great Plague of 1665, smoking was made compulsory at a school called Eton. (You might have heard of it – lots of prime ministers went there, for some reason. Maybe they had special lessons in how to be a prime minister?) The doctors of the day thought that the smoke would somehow fight off the plague, which they decided was floating around in the air. Pupils at the school who refused to smoke would get hit with a cane by their teachers. The olden days were **WEIRD**.

CRAZY CURES

You know how sometimes a good idea actually turns out to be a really, really, really bad one? Like when I was eight and had the excellent idea to slide down the pavement using home-made ice skates, and then suddenly found myself in hospital with an elbow pointing the wrong way and a big red hole where my tooth used to be. Well, a hundred years ago, doctors came up with a brand-new medicine to stop people coughing called heroin. It worked! And then . . . everyone got addicted to it and couldn't stop taking it, and it caused terrible side effects, including the very worst side effect of all. (I mean death, not farting.) You might have heard of heroin because it's now a totally illegal drug.

The Chapter Where

NO ONE WASHES THEIR HANDS

&

A HAIRDRESSER CUTS YOUR LEG OFF

(also known as SURGERY)

IF YOU'VE EVER SEEN AN OPERATION (hopefully from watching something gory on TV rather than breaking into a hospital and sitting on a surgeon's shoulders), then you'll know that surgery is very sophisticated, extremely precise and super clean. It may not be the biggest shock in the world to find out that this hasn't always been the case. First of all, it's very difficult to repair something if you don't know how it's meant to work – and doctors didn't have a clue about how the body works until ages after they started attempting operations. It's a bit like if I tried to get Pippin to fix my computer – she'd have a go, but it wouldn't really help. (And she'd probably wee on it.)

Secondly, they didn't have anaesthetics to make patients fall asleep, and if they had any painkillers at all they were pretty basic.

This meant an operation might go a bit like this:

It was probably pretty distracting if your patient was fighting you off and wailing like they were being murdered. And even if you somehow managed to do a successful operation despite all this, the patient would probably still be killed by an infection. The poor surgeon – doing all that work only for their patient to die because antibiotics hadn't been invented yet. Oh yeah, and it was pretty bad news for the patient too, I guess. Thankfully, things got more advanced over the years. I'm really glad my tonsils weren't removed using a sharpened rock and no anaesthetic.

Might have taught you a lesson. Prunella

ANCIENT EGYPT

In Ancient Egypt, they were extremely good at stitching skin and used all sorts of different materials to do it, from cotton (fair enough) to bits of muscles that they'd pulled out of animals (not fair enough). Thankfully, they saved their sewing skills for people who'd already died: it was mostly to make mummies' bodies look nice and neat for the afterlife, just as soon as they'd cut them open and scooped out all their organs.

We know that they also tried some more advanced surgery because it was described in a document called the Edwin Smith Papyrus. (I presume Edwin Smith is the name of the bloke who found it or something. Most Ancient Egyptian people I've heard of were called things like Cleopatra or Tutankhamun – Edwin Smith sounds more like the name of a maths teacher.) There are lots of descriptions in Edwin's papyrus of operating on spinal injuries and removing lumps, but not many descriptions about how the patients got on afterwards. My guess would be . . . not great. It also said that you should spread some honey on the patient's skin to clean it before an operation (this might work), that you can stop a wound bleeding by putting a lump of raw meat on it (this probably won't work) and if your operation isn't successful, then you should just do a magic spell (this definitely won't work).

ANCIENT INDIA

A thousand years later, in about 600 BC, a man in India called Sushruta invented a whole load of operations. In fact, he invented so many operations that he became known as the Father of Surgery. (I hope Sushruta isn't reading this because I don't want to upset him or make him feel less important, but I've just looked up 'the Father of Surgery' on Wikipedia, and there are literally ten other people in history who have been called that. Actually, I've just looked Sushruta up on Wikipedia too and he died 2,500 years ago, so he's definitely not reading this.)

He wrote a book with 184 chapters (184! This book only has twelve!), which described how to do all sorts of things, from amputating an arm to making someone a new nose if it had been chopped off in a sword fight. His method involved cutting off the patient's cheek and turning that into a nose. Presumably, he then had to cut off something else to replace the missing cheek? Their bum, maybe?

Can you stop talking about bums? It's not funny, it's not clever, and it makes me embarrassed to be related to you. Prunella

ANCIENT ROME

In Ancient Rome, they developed an operation called a Caesarean section, which was a new way of delivering a baby through the abdomen (which is what doctors call the tummy because we like having weird names for stuff). Fancy a quick game? It's true or false, and if you lose you have to buy me a helicopter. True or false . . . the Caesarean section is called the Caesarean section because Julius Caesar was born by one?

Nope! False! You owe me a helicopter. (Can I have it in bright green, please, with ADAM'S LOVELY HELICOPTER in gold writing on the side? Thanks.) It might start with the name 'Caesar', but it's got nothing to do with old Julius. It was impossible for a mother to survive a Caesarean in those days, and Mummy Caesar (I'm not sure what her first name was – Julia, maybe?) was still alive when Julius was grown up.

YOU CAN INVADE BRITAIN ONCE YOU'VE TIDIED YOUR ROOM!

AL-ZAHRAWI

It's time to say hi to Abu al-Qasim Khalaf ibn al-Abbas al-Zahrawi al-Ansari, although I hope you don't mind if I shorten his name to al-Zahrawi. He lived in the year 1000 (I wonder if they had a big party to celebrate the year 1000?) and was a pretty amazing surgeon. He invented a type of stitch made from the intestines of cats (which – slightly disgustingly – is sometimes still used today). As well as that, he made over two hundred different types of instruments for surgeons (I mean like scalpels, not saxophones) and described lots of brand-new operations. Oh, and also he wrote about thirty books and invented loads of different perfumes.

All right, al-Zahrawi.

Nobody likes a show-off.

SPARKLE TIME

In Sparkle Time (you know what I mean), doctors weren't into the idea of surgery that much. Maybe they were worried that some blood would splash onto their shoes or something. Whatever the reason, they stuck to their leeches and lotions and potions, and pretty much refused to pick up a scalpel. So – what happened if you really, really needed an operation? Well, you went to the hairdresser's. It made sense in a way – they were already using knives and scissors for their normal job, so they didn't need to buy any new equipment.

Even though it must have been very handy to have a quick haircut and your leg amputated at the same time, the downsides were that anaesthetics hadn't been invented, doctors weren't very good at stopping things bleeding, and you'd probably get an infection afterwards and die. But at least you'd have a lovely neat hairdo for the funeral.

If you look outside a barber's shop today, you might see a pole with red and white stripes on it. Do you know why that is? It's in tribute to their favourite yoghurt:

Strawberry Fruit Corner. Hmm, maybe not. It's meant to look like a white bandage covered in blood, which told everyone walking past that they did operations. I'd have gone for something less off-putting, like a nice pair of scissors, maybe. The whole blood-on-bandages thing is a bit like a restaurant having a picture of a vomit splat outside.

That's disgusting — please delete that sentence. And the rest of the chapter too. Prunella

One of the most famous barber-surgeons (as they were known) was called Ambroise Paré. Not to be confused with Framboise Pâté, which is French for raspberry jelly.

AMBROISE PARÉ: FIVE FACTS AND A LIE

1. He was the official doctor to four French kings in a row. You only get a new king when the last one dies, so they probably should have found a better doctor.

2. He was taught how to do surgery by his brother. My brother taught me how to make a fart sound by putting my hand under my armpit, which is almost as good. (Did you just check if you could do it?)

3. If someone had been poisoned in the olden days, doctors would make them eat a bezoar stone to cure them. (A bezoar is a kind of stone that sometimes appears in the gut. Yuck.) Ambroise proved that these poo-stones weren't actually any good at treating poisons. Unfortunately, he proved it by poisoning his cook and showing that he still died despite eating a bezoar afterwards. Naughty Ambroise.

4. He once survived an attempted murder by hiding in a wardrobe.

5. He invented forensic pathology, which means working out how someone was murdered. There are TV shows about forensic pathology called things like **CSI: Miami.** (His TV show would be called **CSI: Sixteenth-century Paris.**)

6. Paris was named after him.

One of Ambroise's big inventions was a way of using stitches to stop blood vessels from bleeding everywhere during surgery (although he may have stolen the idea from al-Zahrawi). Previously, doctors would use an extremely hot bit of metal to sizzle and seal the bleeding blood vessels like they were cooking a steak. This had the unfortunate result of killing a lot of patients, so

Because a lot more of his patients lived to tell the (slightly gruesome) tale of their amputations, he developed prosthetic or artificial limbs for them to use afterwards. He also made artificial eyes for people who had lost theirs, usually in battles. You couldn't see through them, but they were made out of gold or silver, so they must have looked pretty amazing.

→ Ambroise's method was much better and a lot more people survived their operations. They were also less likely to die of an infection afterwards, thanks to an ointment he developed made of egg yolk and rose oil. (I'm not sure how he discovered this. Maybe he was making custard one day and some mixture splashed onto a patient.)

Not only was he a decent surgeon, he wrote a book of all his various tips, tricks and life hacks. (They were mostly actual hacks, using a saw.) Normally, textbooks were written in Latin, which meant you had to be very posh to understand them, but Ambroise decided to write his in French so it was easy for all the other surgeons to learn from him. This improved the quality of operations throughout France. Merci beaucoup, Ambroise!

MISTER LISTER AND SOME DIRTY BLISTERS

If you had to have an operation, where would you rather have it – in a hospital, or on your kitchen table? If you lived around two hundred years ago, then the answer would be, 'Definitely at home, please. Please, please, please, please, please!' because patients were five times more likely to die in hospital. Why? Well, let me describe how surgeons did their operations in hospital and see if you can work it out.

Unlike surgeons now, who wear special hygienic outfits that look like pyjamas and get thoroughly washed after every operation, surgeons in those days never bothered changing their clothes between operations – they dressed in a black suit with a flowing cape, like they were doing an impression of Dracula. (It was actually a very good impression of Dracula because they killed a lot of people.)

They didn't clean the operating table, or their scalpels, or **ANYTHING**. They didn't even wipe them down – they just used them on the next patient straight away. They even reused blood-soaked bandages. Ugh.

They thought that if at the end of the day you were covered head to toe in blood and intestines and poo and pus and vomit and bits of brain and splinters of bone then it meant you were a really good surgeon. If you're in Cubs or Scouts, you collect different badges; these guys would collect different types of innards all over their clothes. Just like Pippin doesn't think she's been for a proper walk unless she's rolled in ten different kinds of fox poo.

They didn't wear gloves and they never washed their hands. Ever.

Yep, even **YOU** worked out the answer and you're only three/four/five/six/seven/eight/nine/ten/eleven/twelve/thirteen/fourteen/eighty-six (*delete as appropriate*). But surgeons back then had no idea why everyone was dying of infection – they thought infections just spread through the air, and were nothing to do with their hideous blood-soaked hands and clothes.

Well, they did until the 1800s when a bloke called Joseph Lister came along. He'd heard of a substance called carbolic acid, which was a sort of old-school bleach that cities used to make their sewers less stinky. He thought it might be a good idea if surgeons washed all their instruments in carbolic acid, as well as giving the operating theatre a wipe-down with it, and wore clean gloves for every operation. He tried this in his hospital and the death rates suddenly plummeted.

Surgeons up and down the country were delighted! No, not delighted – furious. A medical journal called the *Lancet* (like a really boring comic for doctors) told every single surgeon that they should ignore Lister's weird idea of 'washing things'. The *Lancet* (which is still printed today) said he didn't know what he was talking about, and all this cleaning would slow down their operations. I think the truth was that they didn't want to look stupid, or admit that they were wrong. Like when I tried to dye my hair blond, but it somehow went this ridiculous green colour, so I pretended to everyone that it was deliberate and that I wanted it to be that colour all along.

Luckily, a few years later, everyone realized that Lister was right after all, and they started using his techniques. Which is excellent news if you're ever time-travelling to the nineteenth century and your appendix bursts.

Your hair looks ridiculous whatever colour it is. Prunella

ANAESTHETICS: FROM AAAAAAAAAGH TO ZZZZZZZZ

Surgeons have known for thousands of years that it's not **GREAT** for people to be awake and screaming during their operations: it's hard to operate on someone when they're flapping about, and it's probably not a whole load of fun for the patient either. They tried all sorts of things, like giving the patient so much alcohol that they fell asleep, or smashing them on the head until they were unconscious, or even hypnotizing them. Unfortunately, these things either didn't work, or made the patients a bit too dead.

In the 1830s, there was a craze for university students to go to parties and breathe in a newly discovered type of gas called ether. One day a doctor called Crawford Long noticed that students who'd been breathing in ether and then injured themselves didn't feel any pain . . . and he wondered if this gas might be useful for when he was doing operations. (He was right – it was extremely useful.)

One of the first-ever operations that took place with ether as an anaesthetic was the amputation of a man's leg. It went so well that the patient asked when the operation was going to begin, but his leg was already in the bin and he hadn't felt a thing.

Other surgeons were very suspicious of ether, and said that an operation couldn't work properly if the patient didn't feel any pain during it . . . eek! But since then millions and millions of operations have been performed using anaesthetics, although today doctors use different types of gas because ether had this annoying habit of sometimes exploding. Oops.

To this day, doctors have no idea how anaesthetics actually work (idiots!), but the main thing is that they **DO** work, and operations are a lot less screamy than they used to be.

BEFORE

AFTER

1846

Before anaesthetics were invented, a surgeon's best chance of not killing their poor screaming patient was to do the operation extremely quickly. The fastest surgeon in Britain was a man called Robert Liston, who boasted that he could amputate a leg in less than a minute. In 1846, Mr Liston did an operation so quickly that he killed the patient with a clumsy swish of his knife **and then** he killed his assistant by accidentally cutting off his fingers **AND THEN** he killed someone who was watching the operation, who died of fright. Whoops!

LEND A HAND (OR A LUNG OR A KIDNEY)

I've talked a bit about transplants already – the amazing operations to give people a new heart or lungs or even a new hand or a new bum. OK, I made up the bum bit. Doctors have wanted to do transplants for thousands of years, but they've only actually happened quite recently. So why did it take so long? Were they all just really lazy? Or did they keep putting it off, like the way you're always far too busy to tidy your bedroom?

The reason that it took surgeons *soooo* long to transplant an organ is that, when they tried it, the patients just died. Even if they put it in exactly the right place and

→ Then why did you put it in? This book is totally unsuitable for children. I hope they all have bins at home. Prunella

connected it up perfectly to all the complicated veins and arteries . . . the patient still ended up totally dead. This was because of something called organ rejection. Your body is so marvellous and miraculous that as soon as something appears inside that it doesn't recognize, it goes straight on the attack. This is excellent news if you have an illness because the viruses or bacteria or other evil invaders get zapped and destroyed. But it's not quite so handy if you're trying to install a new organ.

The big change happened when scientists invented a drug that stops the immune system (the part of the body that fights infections) from getting overexcited, which means the body doesn't try to boot out its lovely new replacement organ. This drug was invented by an incredible scientist called Gertrude Elion – she won a Nobel Prize for it, and fair enough really.

Because their immune systems have been turned right down, it's really important that people with organ transplants stay away from people who are ill because they're not as good at fighting off germs.

The twentieth century saw a lot of firsts: the first kidney transplant (1954) …

… the first liver transplant (1967) …

… the first heart transplant (1967) …

… the first heart and lung transplant (1981) …

… and first place in the egg-and-spoon race (me, at sports day in 1987). I'm sure you'll agree that the egg-and-spoon race was the main highlight.

You came last in that race. Stop lying. Prunella

FANTASTIC PLASTIC

What's plastic surgery? I'll give you three options:

1. Having Lego stitched to your face.

2. An operation to change the shape of things like your nose or your lips.

3. Surgery to restore the face or body after major burns, injuries or operations.

If you said 2 or 3, then you'd be right. If you said 1, then go and sit in a dustbin full of fish for an hour. The word plastic means 'reshaping', and it's a much older meaning of the word than the stuff bags and containers and plugs are made of. Just like the word poo-breath was around for years before I started calling Pippin that.

Doctors have been attempting plastic surgery on patients' faces for thousands of years, ever since Sushruta started making new noses. As well as losing them in sword fights (*aagh!*), there were also infections that ate away at people's faces (*aaaaagh!*) that doctors tried to repair over the years.

I'M OVER HERE!

Like most kinds of surgery, there wasn't a lot doctors could do until anaesthetics came along. But, even when patients could snooze through their operations, doctors didn't have much experience doing them, so very little plastic surgery got performed. This all changed about a hundred years ago, during the First World War. (Although I guess they didn't know it was called the First World War at the time, unless a friendly time-traveller had told them about the Second World War.)

2010
Doctors in Spain performed the first face transplant on a man whose (original) face got very badly damaged in a shooting accident. If you receive a face transplant, you still look more like your old self than the person whose new face you've got. This is because what you look like is more to do with the bones underneath than the skin on top. Some mornings I look at myself in the mirror and wonder if someone has secretly transplanted Pippin's face onto my head overnight, but I normally look a bit better after a shower and a quick shave.

Barely. Prunella

During the war, sadly, a lot of people were injured – and so many soldiers had injuries to their faces and hands from gunshots or explosions that in 1917 a whole hospital was set up in England to look after them. The doctors, led by a genius called Harold Gillies, performed over 11,000 operations on these soldiers, and basically invented all the techniques of plastic surgery that are still used today. During the Second World War they made the amazing discovery that pilots whose planes crashed in the water healed much better than pilots whose planes crashed on land. This taught them that using salt water on wounds could save a lot of lives.

THROUGH THE KEYHOLE

If someone collapses at home and they need an urgent operation, but the surgeons can't open the door to get to them, they do something called keyhole surgery from their front doorstep.

OK, fine. That might not be one hundred per cent true. Keyhole surgery (or laparoscopy, if you're a show-off who prefers much longer words) is actually what it's called when doctors don't make a big cut to do an operation, but instead make a few tiny holes: one to look inside with a mini camera, and a couple more to put little grabbers and cutters and stitchers inside.

Think of it like removing a crisp from a packet. The old-fashioned way is to rip the packet right open and pluck out a delicious slice of fried potato. The keyhole surgery method would be to make a couple of little holes in the packet and use chopsticks to break up the crisp into tiny pieces, then remove it all from one of the holes. No one would ever know if you stole one of their crisps! (But, on the downside, your crisp would be all smooshed up.)

Laparoscopy means the person having the operation recovers faster and feels less pain afterwards, and they don't end up with such a big scar. The downsides of this type of operation are that they often take a bit longer, and laparoscopy is quite complicated to spell. I won't lie to you – I've relied quite heavily on autocorrect to write this section. Also, you might be the kind of weirdo who wants to show off a massive scar to your friends.

The first-ever laparoscopy was carried out in 1901 by a German doctor called Georg Kelling who performed it on a dog. (Don't read this bit, Pippin!) Luckily, it all went well and he wrote in his notes that the dog was 'as cheerful as it was before'. How did he know? Maybe the dog told him a joke?

A dog could write better jokes than you, Prunella

2001

A patient in France had her gall bladder removed by some surgeons who were halfway across the world in New York. No, they didn't have really long scissors that reached right across the ocean. The patient had a three-armed machine moving its scalpel-ended arms around inside her, while her doctors were waggling its controls four thousand miles away. Luckily, the Wi-Fi didn't go down, and the operation was a success. Please don't have any nightmares about a three-armed machine with scalpel-ended arms performing surgery on you.

THE FUTURE

And now some more predictions from my robot butler. He's just been washing the car. (Unfortunately, he put it in the shower and destroyed my bathroom.)

PREDICTION 1 — SURGEONS WILL ALL BE REPLACED BY ROBOTS.

Hopefully not my robot butler though, because he can't even make toast without burning it. But robots will be doing almost every operation; and there won't even be any doctors controlling them; they'll just get on with it on their own. The good news is they'll be a lot faster at operating than humans, and much more accurate, which will make surgery even safer.

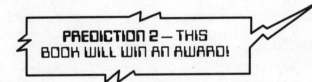

PREDICTION 2 — THIS BOOK WILL WIN AN AWARD!

That's wonderful news – thank you! I'll get my suit dry-cleaned for the ceremony.

PREDICTION 3 — THE AWARD IS FOR WORST BOOK OF THE YEAR.

Oh.

ADAM'S ANSWERS

WHAT HAPPENS IF YOU NEED AN OPERATION IN THE ANTARCTIC?

It's not an ideal place to require emergency surgery because there aren't any hospitals, so most expeditions bring a doctor along in case there are any serious issues. But what if the doctor needs an operation? This happened in 1961 to a Russian doctor called Leonid Rogozov, who realized he had appendicitis when he was at the South Pole. It would have been impossible to get to a hospital in time to save his life, so the only solution was for him to do the operation himself, and cut out his own appendix! He lay down and cut into his abdomen while other people passed him equipment and held up mirrors so he could see what he was doing. Amazingly, the operation was a success and he made a full recovery.

WHAT WAS THE LARGEST THING EVER REMOVED DURING AN OPERATION?

In 1991, a woman had a tumour removed from her ovary that weighed 130 kilograms. That's about the same weight as a large panda, or twenty-five bowling balls or eight hundred avocados. Basically, it was massive.

CAN DOCTORS DO HEAD TRANSPLANTS?

No.

Oh, did you want a longer answer than that? OK, well, scientists have managed to transplant a rat's head onto a different rat's body. (Or at least they claim they did – all rats look kind of the same to me, so they might have just splashed a bit of blood on its neck and pretended they did the operation.) They've never attempted it on a human – partly because no one's sure if it'll actually work, and partly because (strangely enough) there aren't many people volunteering to have their heads chopped off for an experiment. (My lawyer, Nigel, has asked me to point out that you shouldn't volunteer for a head transplant.)

TRUE OR POO?

IT'S POSSIBLE TO DO OPERATIONS ON BABIES BEFORE THEY'RE BORN.

TRUE Sometimes scans on a pregnant mum show that the baby has a problem with its heart, lungs or spinal cord that needs an operation. Doctors can perform this surgery when the baby is still inside the uterus, many weeks before it's born. Amazingly, these babies heal so quickly that they're born without a scar. Aren't humans amazing? (Especially me.)

→ *Nope. Prunella*

THE WORLD RECORD FOR THE MOST SURGERY WAS A MAN WHO HAD NINETY-SEVEN SEPARATE OPERATIONS.

POO It was a lot more than that! The world record is an American man who had NINE HUNDRED AND SEVENTY operations – so, nearly a thousand! He had a rare condition that meant he developed lots of lumps on his skin that needed to be removed. I hope he had some kind of loyalty card that got him a free coffee with every tenth operation.

DOCTORS USED TO TRANSPLANT FROG SKIN ONTO HUMANS.

TRUE Some of the earliest attempts at skin transplantation used animal skin. Doctors did experiments using monkeys, goats and dogs (sorry, Pippin!) but they didn't go very well – plus, they must have left patients with random hairy patches of skin. One doctor treated a child who had bad burns by using frog skin, and . . . it was a success! Unfortunately, the boy didn't end up with cool slimy green patches on his body – it blended in with his own skin pretty quickly. Boring!

CRAZY CURES

Been wounded in battle? Sorry to hear that. If it happened in the seventeenth century, your doctor's first question would probably be to ask if you've got the sword that attacked you. They would then make a delicious paste out of some old rust and ground-up worms and rub it on the sword because they thought that would heal the wound. You don't have to be the biggest genius in the history of geniuses to work out that this was a load of absolute nonsense.

AND IS THIS THE SWORD YOU WERE ATTACKED WITH?

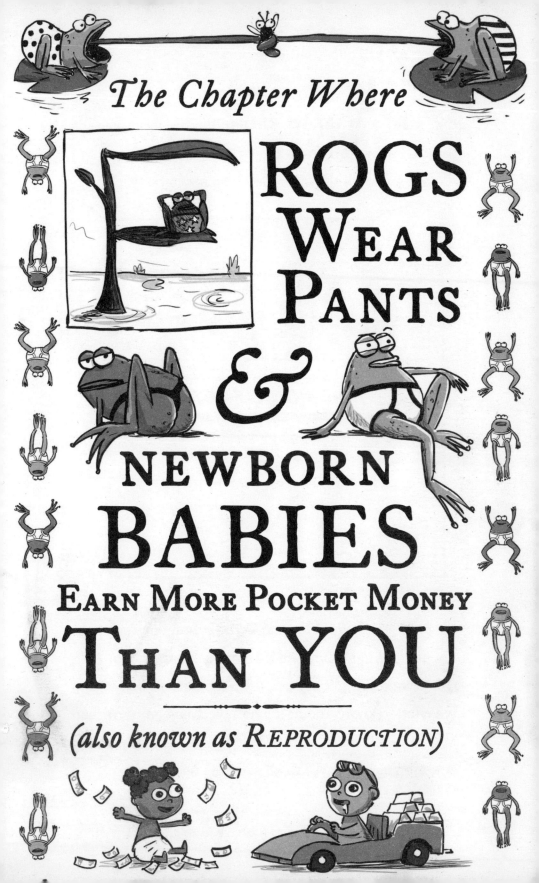

The Chapter Where

FROGS WEAR PANTS

&

NEWBORN BABIES EARN MORE POCKET MONEY THAN YOU

(also known as REPRODUCTION)

OK, HERE'S WHAT WE KNOW. Reproduction means that a male sperm joins forces with a female egg and around nine months later they turn into a baby.

It's obviously slightly unexpected when you first hear about how it all happens. I was a bit like, '*Riiiiight,* OK . . .' and you might have been too. But it's something we need to know about. It's nothing to be embarrassed by – after all, we're all grown-ups here. Actually, you're not, are you? Well, we're all sensible people.

You're clearly not a sensible person, Adam, so that sentence is a lie. Delete it. Prunella

Because sperms and eggs are a bit on the really, really, really tiny side, you can only see them with a microscope and there was a *looooooooooooong* time when we didn't have microscopes so no one knew what was going on. So what did they do?

1. Say, 'No idea what's happening here – let's just ignore it for a few centuries until someone else works it out.'

2. Make up a load of absolutely ridiculous gibberish.

You'll be delighted to hear the answer is 2.

ANCIENT EGYPT

The Ancient Egyptians thought that a baby was nothing to do with its mum: they reckoned all the woman did was grow the baby, like some kind of person-shaped plant pot, and the child would be a miniature version of its dad.

Their proof for this was that they said dung beetles were all male and they had loads of kids. (They were wrong, by the way – dung beetles aren't only male. Maybe it's just difficult to tell boy beetles from girl beetles? Fun fact: they're called dung beetles because that's what they eat – poo! Maybe Pippin should be called a socks-and-puddle dog.)

OOH. A THREE-COURSE MEAL!

The Ancient Egyptians also had a way of finding out if they were soon going to be a mummy. No, not the kind with bandages – the kind who tells you to eat your broccoli. The possibly pregnant person would wee into a bag of wheat seeds and if the seeds started to sprout this would mean they were pregnant. Strangely, scientists have tested this out recently, and it actually works!

ANCIENT GREECE

If I asked you what the uterus was for, you'd tell me it's where a baby grows. But if you asked someone in Ancient Greece they'd tell you that it was a creature with a life of its own that constantly moved around a woman's body like an out-of-control drone. Umm . . . If a woman had almost anything wrong with her, the Ancient Greeks would say it was because of her 'wandering womb' going for a cheeky float about. Feeling dizzy? The womb's gone up too high. Trouble speaking? The womb's too low. And the treatment was to use different smells to move the uterus back to its usual place . . . sweet smells to lure it nearer and revolting smells to make it go further away. Please wait a second while I sigh really loudly. OK, we can move on now.

FUN UTERUS MAZE! GUIDE THE LOST WOMB BACK HOME

Long before ultrasound was invented, people were very interested in whether their baby was going to be a boy or a girl – probably so they could think about what name to call it.

Old Hippoface thought that if a woman got spots on her skin while she was pregnant then she'd have a girl and if her skin stayed clear then she'd have a boy. What a load of dung (as they'd say in Ancient Egypt).

Remember how I said that women didn't use to be allowed to work as doctors because of something called sexism? Well, see if you can spot any other examples of sexism in this chapter. Clue: there are **LOADS** of them. In the fourth century BC, a Greek woman called Agnodice thought this was very unfair because she knew she'd be a great doctor, so she disguised herself as a man and sneaked into medical school. She specialized in obstetrics, which means delivering babies, and was the type of doctor I used to work as – it's a really fun type of medicine because you start with one patient, and you end up with two! Agnodice was brilliant at her job and helped hundreds of women. Unfortunately, the male doctors found out her secret and she was arrested and put on trial. Luckily, the women she'd treated came to her defence, and she was let off. Hooray! And then they changed the law to say that women throughout Greece could be doctors too. Double hooray!

Shockingly, in Britain, women weren't allowed to be doctors until 1865, when Elizabeth Garrett Anderson first picked up her stethoscope.

ELIZABETH GARRETT ANDERSON: FIVE FACTS AND A LIE

1. Because no universities would let her train as a doctor, she signed up for a nursing course, but secretly went into the doctors' lectures instead.

2. Even though she eventually qualified as a doctor, no hospital would give her a job, so she set up her own one. Basically, she was a woman who wouldn't take no for an answer.

3. To make it easier for other women to become doctors, her hospital only employed women.

4. Her sister, Millicent Fawcett, was one of the main people who got the law changed so that women could vote – what an amazing family. (My family is amazing too: I'm the cleverest man in the world and my sister can burp 'Happy Birthday'.)

5. Elizabeth later became the country's first-ever female mayor.

6. Even later, she became the first-ever woman to walk on the moon.

6. No one was stomping around in space in the nineteenth century. And, even though twelve astronauts have walked on the moon so far, none of them have been women. Maybe you or someone you know will be the first? Let me know!

ANCIENT ROME

A quick reminder: the male reproductive system involves things on the outside like a penis and testicles; the female reproductive system has got things on the inside like a vagina, uterus and ovaries. Two pretty different set-ups, right? Well, you'd disagree if you lived in Ancient Rome – they believed that these were exactly the same thing. Yes, you did read that right: they thought the vagina was a penis that was turned inside out, and the ovaries were exactly the same as testicles. They didn't even give ovaries their own name: they were just known as 'female testicles'. Galen said:

WOMEN HAVE EXACTLY THE SAME ORGANS AS MEN, BUT IN EXACTLY THE WRONG PLACES.

(That's right, Pippin – it's definitely another example of sexism.)

Next up in the massive list of things they got wrong: periods. They thought periods (also known as menstruation, when the lining of the uterus comes out of a girl's vagina once a month after puberty) were evil. I know, I know – they're totally normal and about half of the people in the world have them. But in Ancient Rome they thought that period blood could make plants and animals die. Absolutely ridiculo– Sorry, what's that loud beeping sound? Oh, it's my sexism alarm going off again.

But it wasn't all bad news. A man called Soranus (which hopefully wasn't pronounced 'sore anus') wrote a book with a lot of handy hints about how to help a woman give birth. This became the first-ever textbook for midwives, who are the experts in looking after pregnant mothers and helping them give birth safely. I'd make a **FEW** changes to his textbook, to be honest. For instance, the part where he says that it's dangerous for a pregnant woman to have a bath. Not much fun for the pregnant person – or for anyone they hang out with either!

SPARKLE TIME

When girls or women have their period every month, it can cause pain – and this has been the case forever. Today they can just take painkillers if it gets bad, but this wasn't the case back in Sparkle Time. You might think this was because pain relief hadn't been invented yet, but actually . . . it had! Men would chew on the bark of a willow tree, which sounds a bit weird, but it was effective, and it's where we get a modern medicine called aspirin from. Even though men were allowed pain relief, women weren't. Sorry, I can barely hear myself think – my sexism alarm is going off louder than ever.

NO WOMEN

In the fifteenth century, there was a very popular book called *The Distaff Gospels*, which was full of useful advice for pregnant women. Or so they thought – it was actually as useful as getting Pippin to paint the ceiling. Advice included:

- It's dangerous to eat fruit – umm, pretty bad advice there.

- Don't eat fish heads or your baby's mouth will be too pointy – who even eats fish heads anyway?!

I do, and they're delicious. Prunella

FROGS IN PANTS

I know what you're thinking – you've nearly read a whole book, and not once have I talked about scientists putting a pair of pants on a frog. Well, the wait is finally over, thanks to Lazzaro Spallanzani, who you might remember was the bloke who discovered all about stomach acid.

(Or you might have read that chapter in a hurry. Or you might be reading this book back to front because you're wacky like that. Or your pet lion might have eaten the first half of the book because you were out of raw steaks. There are lots of possible reasons.)

Lazzaro wondered if you needed both a biological mum and a biological dad to have a baby so he came up with a little experiment. He went off to the eighteenth-century version of Marks & Spencer and bought some XXXXXS size pants, which he handed out to a load of frogs. He discovered that if either mum frog or dad frog was wearing pants, there wouldn't be any baby frogs.

This was such an important discovery that there's now a statue of Lazzaro Spallanzani, in his home town of Scandiano, of him looking at a frog through a magnifying glass. Unfortunately, only one of them is wearing pants. (It's Spallanzani.)

1739

Labour (when a woman pushes a baby out at the end of pregnancy) doesn't often last more than a day – but, in Ireland in 1739, a patient called Alice O'Neal had been in labour for twelve days. Her midwife, Mary Donally, decided to perform a Caesarean section to save her life. There were two slight problems here. First of all, Caesareans are usually done by doctors, not midwives, and there weren't any doctors for miles around. And, secondly, no doctor had ever performed this operation successfully before. But there weren't any other options, so Mary took a razor and some needles and thread used for mending clothes and did the operation. Alice survived, which is very impressive – not just because Mary was kind of making up the operation as she went along, but because this was before the invention of anaesthetics or antibiotics.

STINKY SURGEONS

In the nineteenth century, it was very dangerous to have a baby. Many women died because they lost loads of blood during childbirth (luckily, we have drugs now that make that very unlikely to happen) and lots of others died of something called puerperal fever. No, I didn't spell purple wrong: puerperal means they've just had a baby. These women would develop an unexplained fever that they sadly never recovered from.

In 1847, a Hungarian doctor called Ignaz Semmelweis thought he would investigate why this was happening. There were two wards in his hospital where mums gave birth: one run by midwives and one run by doctors. Almost all the cases of puerperal fever were in the doctors' ward. Hmm. Why don't you put a detective hat on your head and a detective pipe in your mouth and see if you can work out what was going on? (My lawyer, Nigel, has asked me to mention that you absolutely shouldn't smoke a pipe.)

Semmelweis's first thought was that a priest often went through the doctors' ward, ringing a bell, to visit someone who had died, so he wondered if the bell was causing puerperal fever. He banned the priest's bell, and what do you think happened? Yep – nothing. Then he noticed that the patients on the midwives' ward gave birth lying in a different position, so he insisted that everyone gave birth in the same position. And how many lives were saved? Yep – none. Finally, he realized that before the doctors turned up to work on this ward they spent a few hours cutting up dead bodies, then started delivering babies without even washing their hands first.

EVERYBODY RUN!
HE'S GOT A BELL!

And there we go! But because Joseph Lister hadn't come along yet with his crazy idea about hand-washing, no one realized this was dangerous. I know, right? Ignaz thought that the dead bodies were leaving a dangerous smell on the doctors' hands, which wasn't quite right, but he came up with the right answer – to wash them! The doctors did this and immediately women stopped dying of puerperal fever. And all the patients in the hospital lived happily ever after.

No, not really. The other doctors started getting upset that they were being accused of making their patients ill, and no one likes to be told they're wrong, especially grumpy old men.

GRUMPY OLD MEN

Ignaz got the sack from the hospital and then became so miserable he ended up living in an asylum, where he died in 1865. (And then, a couple of years later, Joseph Lister proved that Ignaz was right all along – *aagh!*)

1847
Going through labour can be pretty painful (to say the least) so you can imagine that the first patient to get an anaesthetic while having a baby would have been extremely grateful. This woman was so astonished and so happy that she named her baby Anaesthesia. Well, I suppose it's better than being called Ouuuuuuuuch Aaaaaaargh.

CHILD STARS

Most babies are born after nine months spent hanging about in the uterus – if they're born much earlier than that, it's called being premature. These days babies can survive being born at six months and even younger, thanks to amazing doctors and nurses, amazing medicine and an amazing invention called the incubator. The incubator is basically a magic box – no, not the kind you might see somebody using to saw their assistant in half, a different kind – that keeps very premature babies alive by helping them feed and breathe, and by protecting and carefully monitoring them.

The incubator was invented in France in 1880, based on a machine that kept baby chicks warm. An American doctor called Martin Couney was visiting France and saw how well they worked, so told his hospital all about them, and how they massively increased the chance that a premature baby would survive. Unfortunately, his hospital wasn't interested – his bosses just did an impression of the 🤷 emoji and said that premature babies were weaklings who weren't supposed to live. They wouldn't buy any incubators. How mean! Luckily, Martin came up with a brilliant (but totally bananas) plan.

When a premature baby was born, he would care for it in an incubator, but not in the hospital . . . in a theme park. His idea was that after people had been on the roller coaster, and before they went off to buy candyfloss, they might fancy paying twenty-five cents to go into his 'Infantorium' to see some tiny babies, and the entrance fee would help him pay back the money he'd borrowed

During the First World War, a Frenchman called Paul Langevin developed a way of working out how far away underwater enemy submarines were. No, this book hasn't turned into *Kay's Marvellous Submarines*. I'm telling you this because, a couple of decades later, doctors realized they could use exactly the same technology – called ultrasound – to look inside people's bodies and see things like brains and bowels and babies. The first photo ever taken of you was probably an ultrasound – I hope you didn't pull any stupid faces.

to buy the incubators. Sounds weird, but amazingly it was a huge success and people flocked to spend their money and see these magical little babies, even though they didn't juggle chainsaws or walk across a tightrope. By doing this, Couney saved the lives of over six thousand babies. Luckily, these days all hospitals have incubators, which is good news for patients, but bad news if you want to see a cute baby after you've staggered off Nemesis.

THE AMAZING SLEEPING FARTING BABIES

LAB BRATS

Just like people go to see their doctor if they have problems with their lungs or their liver or their bones or their brains, sometimes a man's or a woman's reproductive system needs treatment too. Until about forty years ago, if a couple weren't able to have a baby, doctors couldn't do very much. But these days there's a way of getting pregnant called IVF, which stands for in vitro fertilization and means 'fertilization in glass'. It's not a bad description because in IVF the sperm and the eggs are placed together in a glass dish to start to grow for a few days before they're put into the mother's uterus. The first successful IVF on an animal was carried out in 1959 on a rabbit called Carrotface Megabunny, and the first IVF pregnancy in a human was a girl born in 1978 called Louise Brown. (Yes, I did make up the name of the rabbit – the scientists didn't give her a name, and I thought it was unfair that she was nameless.)

THE FUTURE

Let's fire up my robot butler's prediction module once again. He's just pruned the trees (but unfortunately he covered them all with prune juice).

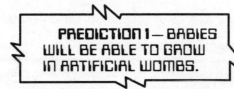

PREDICTION 1 — BABIES WILL BE ABLE TO GROW IN ARTIFICIAL WOMBS.

This is great news for parents who want to go on holiday for nine months until their baby is ready to be born and start screaming and pooing. These artificial wombs will be a bit like fish tanks and will mean that it's much easier to keep an eye on how a baby is growing – you don't need to do a scan if you can just look in through a window. And on the rare occasion that a baby needs an operation before it's born, that would also be much easier to do. Plus, delivering a baby will just be a case of scooping it out with a fishing net or one of those big claws you get at the service station when you're trying to win a prize – no more painful labours or messy Caesarean sections.

PREDICTION 2 — THE NEXT CHAPTER WILL BE EXTREMELY BORING.

Oi! I've got feelings, you know?

How will I be able to tell the difference? Prunella

ADAM'S ANSWERS

WHAT'S A WET NURSE?

No, it's not a nurse whose umbrella broke on the way to hospital. A wet nurse was a woman employed by rich parents to breastfeed their baby because they decided they were too busy and important to do it themselves. These days mums usually breastfeed their own babies, but people who aren't able to, or choose not to, feed them using a bottle. (Of milk, not Cherry Coke.)

CAN YOU FREEZE EGGS?

Yes, but they taste nicer scrambled. Oh, you mean the other kind of eggs. The answer's still yes – they can be safely frozen and used for IVF in the future. Women do this for lots and lots of reasons: for example, before they have treatment such as chemotherapy, which might stop their ovaries working. Also, because eggs disappear with age, some women decide to freeze them when they're younger in case they decide to have children later in life. Oh, and they have to be stored at minus 200°C, so you can't keep them at home, tucked next to your Zoom lollies.

IS IT SAFE FOR PREGNANT WOMEN TO HAVE PETS?

Yes, absolutely, although pet poo can have germs in it, so it's best to avoid pooper-scooping. But in Sparkle Time pets were an absolute no-no. Doctors thought that even looking at an animal would result in a baby being born totally covered in hair. It didn't matter whether a pregnant woman looked at a horse or a hamster, dopey docs thought the memory of this would stick in their brain and a baby would pop out wearing a permanent fleecy onesie.

TRUE OR POO?

YOU CAN ONLY HAVE AN ULTRASOUND WHEN YOU'RE IN THE BATH.

POO Come on – seriously? Ultrasounds in the bath? Utter tripe. But when ultrasound was first invented that was exactly what happened – if a doctor wanted to have a look inside you, they'd chuck you in the tub. This was because ultrasound only works properly if the skin is wet. These days they just put some slimy gel on the part of the body they're scanning. It's much more convenient than running a bath – and makes the hospital's water bill a lot cheaper.

TWINS ARE GETTING MORE COMMON.

TRUE About one in every sixty-five pregnant mums have twins, which is more than ever. There are a couple of reasons for this – firstly, IVF and other treatments that help people get pregnant increase the chance of twins. Secondly, women are having babies later in life than they used to, and this makes it more likely an ovary will randomly decide to release two eggs at once. Do you know any twins? My friend Chris is a twin, but I'm not sure which one is the evil one (there's always an evil one). It's either Chris or his brother, David the Vampire. Probably Chris.

WOMEN USED WEASEL TESTICLES TO STOP THEMSELVES GETTING PREGNANT.

TRUE Well, to **TRY** to stop getting pregnant, that is – I don't think you could really describe this as a successful method. Some historians think that, in Sparkle Time, women would wear a necklace with a pair of weasel testicles dangling from it because doctors believed it prevented pregnancy. Other methods included drinking water with lead in it. This might have actually worked, but unfortunately it also caused a few other minor issues, such as death.

CRAZY CURES

If a woman hasn't gone into labour after nine months, it can become dangerous for the baby. These days we have clever medicines to bring on labour, but in the eighteenth century their methods were a bit stranger (and a lot more useless). Top of the list was smearing the mum with pigeon poo.

Can you stop talking about poo? This is supposed to be a textbook. No one's going to want to read this horrible nonsense. You should go back to being a doctor. Actually, you were probably terrible at that too. Prunella

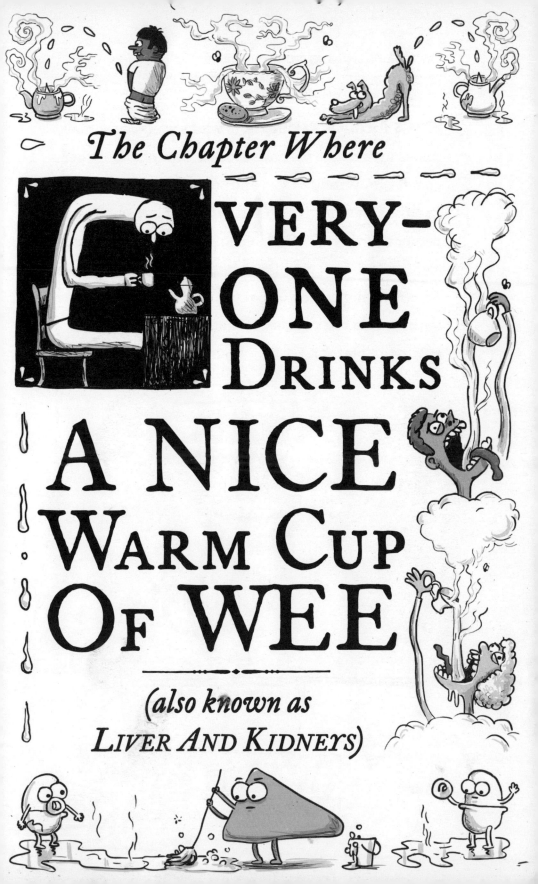

The Chapter Where

EVERY-
ONE Drinks
A NICE
WARM CUP
OF WEE

*(also known as
LIVER AND KIDNEYS)*

HERE'S A QUICK REMINDER of where your wee actually comes from before we have a look at how our forefathers got it so wrong. Oh, and our foremothers and foregrandparents too. Your kidneys filter out waste products from your blood, along with any excess water, and send them off down the ureters to your bladder, and then it finally comes out of your urethra and into the toilet or onto the postman. (That was Pippin, and she's still in trouble for it.)

I think you should mention great aunts here too, otherwise it's very disrespectful. Prunella

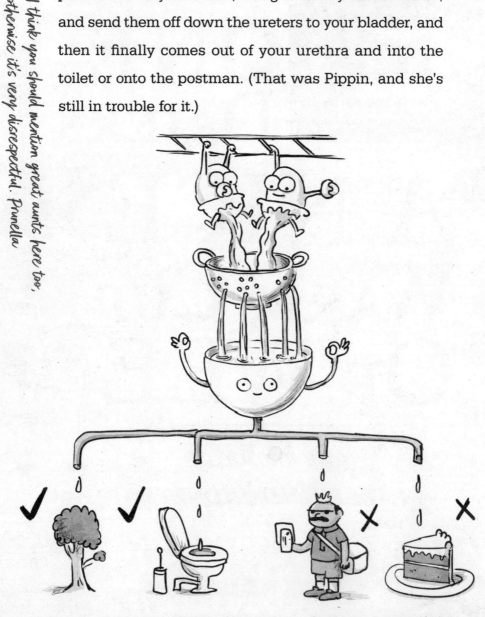

I'll also talk about the liver because I don't want to upset it. A bit like me, it has loads of different jobs. (I'm a writer and a former doctor and a part-time fire juggler.) It's the body's other waste-disposal organ – it takes anything you've eaten or drunk that might be bad for you and turns it into a substance called bile, which it squirts back into the intestine and gives poo its delicious brown colour. Sorry, I mean disgusting brown colour. Please ignore the part where I said poo was delicious.

Luckily, our ancestors have always known exactly what the liver does and how it works. Tricked you! Of course they haven't!

ANCIENT EGYPT

You know when you're not certain about something, but you just have a general vibe about it? Like when you decide not to go for a midnight swim in the lake with the WARNING! DEADLY PIRANHAS! sign on it. Well, the Ancient Egyptians had a vague feeling that the kidneys were pretty important – they just couldn't put their finger on exactly why. The closest they came to an explanation was that the kidneys were advisors to the heart. Advisors?! About what?! Whether to buy a blue T-shirt or a sparkly green one? We'll never know.

But anyway the kidneys were considered important enough to be popped back into mummies' bodies to go off to the afterlife, rather than being sealed in a jar or chucked in the recycling – sorry, brain. They clearly didn't think the liver was especially important though because it ended up with the old jar treatment.

ANCIENT GREECE

In Ancient Greece, they made a wee discovery in the subject of wee medicine – they spotted that it came out of the bladder. Unfortunately, they reckoned that it sort of appeared in the bladder by magic, rather than coming from the kidneys, so they only really get half marks for that. Aristotle was cutting up a fish for dinner one day and spotted that it didn't have any kidneys. He then decided that must mean our kidneys are totally pointless, otherwise fish would need them too. Aristotle clearly wasn't thinking this through, was he? Fish don't have arms or legs either – did he think **THEY** were unnecessary for humans?

The liver had a much better time in Ancient Greece. If this was a textbook back then, at least half of it would be about the liver. They thought the liver was the body's most important organ, and that it was pretty much solely responsible for keeping you alive. (I mean, it's a pretty essential organ, and you definitely wouldn't want your liver to go off on holiday for a fortnight, but I reckon the heart or the brain might have something to say about the whole 'most important' thing.)

They did get something right though, which we know because of a myth they told (myths are like bedtime stories, but all the characters have really long names) about a guy called Prometheus.

Prometheus was the god of fire, and one day he decided to give the people of Earth the gift of . . . you guessed it – fire. I mean, fair enough – he was the god of it. But Zeus, who was the head god – kind of like a head teacher, but even scarier because he could throw bolts of lightning – got extremely cross with him for some reason (maybe he didn't want humans to be able to toast marshmallows) and decided to punish Prometheus. But, instead of sending him to his bedroom or banning him from playing on his Xbox, Zeus chained Prometheus to a rock, where every day an eagle would fly over and peck out his liver. Bit mean, Zeusy. Then the next day Prometheus's liver would reappear . . . but unfortunately so would the eagle.

But what was the important medical fact in there? No, not that eagles love to eat liver for breakfast. The Ancient Greeks worked out that the liver is very good at regenerating – it doesn't happen overnight for us non-gods, but even if the liver gets really badly damaged it can usually sort itself out. Well spotted, Ancient Greeks!

ANCIENT ROME

The Ancient Romans finally worked out that wee comes from the kidneys. I wish they hadn't done it by putting a peg on a monkey's penis, but I promised to tell you how all these discoveries took place, and I'm afraid on this occasion it involved a peg and a monkey's penis. When they did this, the poor monkey couldn't wee for a few days, and its kidneys swelled right up, so they realized that's where the wee was coming from.

AND THEN HE TOOK THE PEG AND PUT IT ON MY . . .

HEY, I'M EATING!

Just like the Ancient Greeks, they were big fans of the liver in Ancient Rome (although I guess they just called it Rome – they didn't know they were ancient). The main thing that they reckoned the liver did was produce the humours. I don't mean they thought the liver was always telling jokes – there's nothing funny about the humours. They were a weird idea that Hippoface came up with in Ancient Greece, which Galen then developed (well, made even weirder) in Rome.

The theory was that every person had four different liquids inside them, and if you had the right amounts of each, then you'd be healthy. On the other hand, if you had too much or too little, then your humours would be all wonky and you'd become unwell. People believed in the humours for thousands of years – in fact, some cultures around the world still base treatments on them.

BLOOD

Fair enough – there's no denying that your body has blood in it. But that's the only tick Galen's homework is going to get. If someone had a fever or was sweating, he reckoned it was because they had too much blood, and so the solution was to let a bit out. Or let a lot out. As you might remember from a few chapters ago, this wasn't really a good idea. (It killed thousands and thousands of people, and didn't help so much as a single headache.)

BLACK BILE

Too much black bile could apparently lead to things like depression. The treatment for this was to make the patient vomit. Unfortunately, they'd still be depressed afterwards, plus now they'd be covered in puke.

YELLOW BILE

The next humour was called yellow bile – too much of this and you'd become angry. The treatment for this was called cupping, where they'd put a load of cups on your skin, suck all the air out and leave them there until you had tons of big red circles all over you. And I do mean **YOU**, because it was also used on people with uncontrollable farting. Some people have cupping today for conditions like back pain, but doctors don't think it actually makes any real difference.

PHLEGM

The fourth humour was phlegm, which is an actual thing that we all have, so I guess they got that one right. As my Great Aunt Prunella says, 'A broken clock is right twice a day' – which means even total idiots get things right sometimes by accident. But they thought it was made in the brain (hmm) and that if there was too much of it going round your body, then snot would pour out of your nose like a broken tap (also hmm – they hadn't heard about colds, I guess). And their cure for too much phlegm? Drink lots of wine. (Biggest hmm yet.)

> That reminds me, I must get batteries for my clock. Prunella

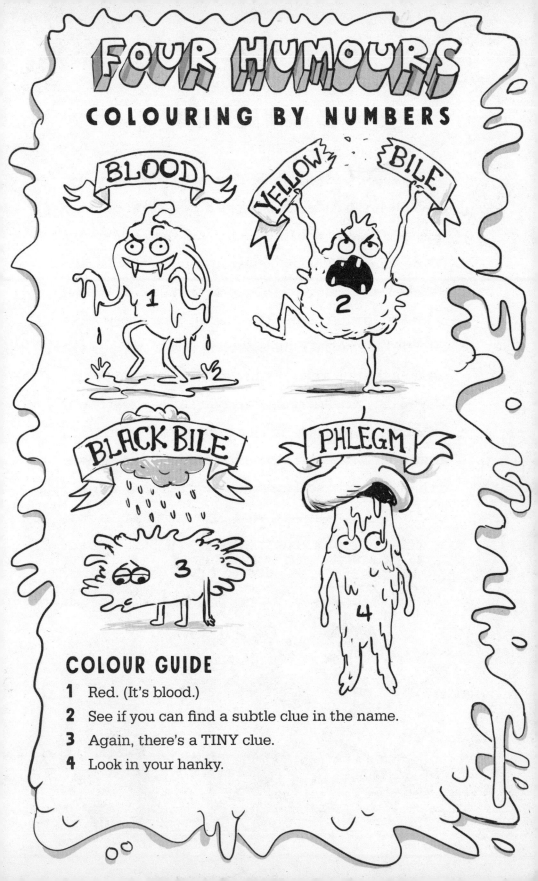

FOUR HUMOURS
COLOURING BY NUMBERS

BLOOD

YELLOW BILE

BLACK BILE

PHLEGM

COLOUR GUIDE

1 Red. (It's blood.)

2 See if you can find a subtle clue in the name.

3 Again, there's a TINY clue.

4 Look in your hanky.

SPARKLE TIME

If we jump ahead to Sparkle Time, they still believed in the humours, but they'd also gone absolutely urine crazy. Honestly, they thought it was the answer to everything. Before doing operations, some surgeons would rinse the patient's skin with wee. (Hopefully they used a bottle of it and a sponge rather than weeing on the patient directly.) Worse than that, doctors would advise their patients to drink a nice warm cup of wee every morning. Maybe they'd heard someone saying 'nice warm cup of tea' and got confused. And if a soldier got shot, then the army's doctors would advise the other soldiers to wee on him. Honestly, as if his day couldn't get any worse.

If I didn't know better, I'd think doctors used to all be sponsored by the Urine Society.

Even though in Europe it was just an extravaganza of people weeing everywhere, over in Iran in the eleventh century, a doctor called Avicenna was making much more important discoveries. He didn't think that wee was a delicious breakfast drink or some kind of antibacterial spray – he realized the yellow stuff was much more important than that.

You know when the doctor sometimes asks you to give a urine sample and you try really, really hard to get it in the pot, but even so most of it goes on the floor. Oh, just me? There are two reasons for that. First of all, the doctor doesn't have any idea what's wrong with you and just wants to get you out of the room for five minutes so he can google 'weird bum rash'. But the second reason is that doctors can use your wee to tell them loads of things about your health. And it was old Avicenna who worked this out.

AVICENNA: FIVE FACTS AND A LIE

1. By the time he was ten, Avicenna had totally memorized the Quran (the main religious book in Islam). That's more than seventy thousand words! By the time I was ten, I was still struggling to tie my shoelaces.

2. When he was eighteen, he was a fully qualified doctor and was already making medical discoveries. In fairness, by the time I was eighteen, I had totally mastered my shoelaces.

3. He recommended dancing as a cure for various illnesses.

4. He wrote his books
   Just like a poem
   I don't know why
   Cos I didn't know him.

5. A copy of his book about the body, *The Canon of Medicine*, sold recently for nearly £200,000. So maybe hold on to this book – it could be worth a fortune (in a thousand years' time).

6. He was put in prison because some important people didn't like the books he'd written.

You should go to prison for this book. I'll visit you every two years. Prunella

3. He didn't prescribe dancing, but he did say that listening to good music was important for staying healthy.

For example, he knew that if your urine was concentrated (I mean a dark colour, not that your wee was thinking very hard) then you needed to drink more water. And if it looked cloudy and smelled really pongy, then it could mean you had an infection. He even worked out that if it was foamy like bubble bath, you might have a problem with your kidneys – all stuff we now know is absolutely true. Top marks, Avicenna! Finally, he worked out that if your urine was purple that meant you were an alien. (There's a tiny chance I made that last bit up.)

URINE SAMPLES

WEE

WHALE WEE

SNOWMAN WEE

ANT WEE

WITCH'S WEE

UNICORN WEE

Avicenna didn't get **EVERYTHING** right though. He wasn't the best at treating some of the illnesses he managed to diagnose. For example, if you had a problem with your kidneys, he would put a load of insects in your pants so they could crawl inside you and somehow sort things out. When you've finished screaming, we can move on to the next section.

NO SENSE OF HUMOUR

Sometimes people say things and everyone just believes them for ages, like when Julian Pringle in my class at school said that his dad was an Olympic sprinter and we all believed him until the next Olympics when there wasn't anyone called Colin Pringle competing in the 100 metres. Doctors believed Galen's theory about the four humours for even longer than we believed Julian Pringle. In fact, no one questioned it for about 1,500 years, until the seventeenth century when William Harvey came along. He was the smarty-pantaloons who figured out circulation, and decided to solve the mystery of the liver too.

Willz had a bit of a fiddle around and discovered that the humours were just a load of made-up old nonsense. (Galen had been dead for a very long time, so he didn't get his head flushed down the toilet, unlike poor Julian Pringle.) He also figured out how the liver worked and how it was connected to other organs around it called the gall bladder and the spleen.

THE DUSTPAN AND BRUSH OF KNOWLEDGE

THE HUMOURS

THE BIN OF HISTORY

THE SOCKS OF TRUTH

DIABETES

You might know someone with diabetes – you might even have it yourself. It's to do with an organ that hangs out next to your liver called the pancreas, which has the very important job of making a substance called insulin that sorts out the levels of sugar in your blood. If your pancreas starts misbehaving, then you get too much sugar sloshing around you and this is called diabetes. But diabetes isn't something new – it's existed for as long as grown-ups have been terrible at dancing (forever).

In Ancient Egypt, they wrote on their dusty papyrus scrolls about an illness that made people go to the toilet a lot and lose weight, which was almost certainly diabetes. Galen got it a bit wrong (classic Galen) and thought it was a problem with the kidneys. However, he did come up with a disgusting name for it: diarrhoea of the urine. The Urine Society must have been very annoyed when the name got changed to diabetes.

A bunch of people had a go at treating diabetes – but they had no idea what was causing it, so their attempts were pretty useless. Over a thousand years ago, a doctor called Paul of Aegina thought he was a bit of a diabetes expert. (Paul seems a very ordinary name for someone from the olden days, doesn't it? I wonder if he had a brother called Steve.)

ELDRON THE WISE

XANDARA SLAYER of DRAGONS

PAUL

His cure? Bloodletting and drinking wine. They seemed to think those things would cure quite a lot of illnesses, didn't they? Turns out they didn't work at all.

But it wasn't until 1675 that this condition was finally given its name. We usually just call it diabetes, but its full name is actually 'diabetes mellitus' – a bit like how we call the queen 'Elizabeth', but most people don't know her surname is actually Bummo. (I may have invented this.) Anyway, mellitus means 'honey', because (please put your milkshake down for this bit) the sugar in diabetic patients' urine makes it taste like honey. Quite how they discovered this in the first place doesn't bear thinking about. Maybe the vending machine was broken in a hospital one day and a particularly thirsty doctor decided to have a quick sip of some urine samples? It took until 1910 to work out what was causing diabetes, when a doctor with the pretty amazing name of Sir Edward Sharpey-Schafer came along. He discovered that people with diabetes didn't produce a certain substance and he named it insulin. (If I was him, I'd have named it Sharpey-Schafer Stuff.)

They weren't any closer to treating diabetes though. In 1919, a doctor called Frederick Allen put his patients with diabetes on a diet of . . . total starvation. (Umm, this doesn't sound like it's going to end well.) It helped a few patients, but most of them starved to death. (Knew it.) Thank goodness then for a couple of doctors called Banting and Best, who sound like a comedy double act, but were actually brilliant scientists who made insulin for the first time. If you're a cow, please stop reading now. The very first insulin injections were made by smooshing up a cow pancreas, and it meant that diabetes could finally be treated. These days, insulin is made in a lab rather than from smooshed-up cow pancreas. Cows, you can start reading again now.

NO BOOZE IS GOOD BOOZE

We all know that drinking too much alcohol is very bad for the liver. Well, if you didn't know that before, then you do now. But for years and years and years doctors didn't just think it was totally fine to drink as much alcohol as you liked – they thought it was really good for you. I've got no idea how they got this so very wrong – maybe they were all drunk?

In Ancient Greece, alcohol was used to treat everything from bad breath to being stabbed in the heart with a sword. (Turns out it made bad breath worse, and wasn't really going to fix the old sword-in-heart situation either.) In Sparkle Time, they thought alcohol was such an important medicine that it was known as 'aqua vitae', which means 'the water of life'. Whether you turned up to the doctor's with a dog bite or an attack of the plague, they'd send you home with a prescription for alcohol. The average adult drank four and a half litres of beer every day in those days – that's the same amount as thirteen cans of Coke. But of beer! *Aaagh!*

It wasn't until 1793 that a doctor called Matthew Baillie finally worked out that alcohol could damage the liver. He published this in a book called *A Series of Engravings, Tending to Illustrate the Morbid Anatomy of Some of the Most Important Parts of the Human Body*. It must have been a massive book to fit all those words on the cover.

1980

There's a condition called kidney stones where the kidneys decide to fill up with stones – maybe it's really boring being a kidney and they need a hobby? – and this can be extremely sore. People have had kidney stones for thousands of years – some mummies even had stones as big as tennis balls rattling around in them! The treatment used to be almost as painful as the stones themselves and involved putting some nutcrackers inside the patient to smash them up. The stones I mean, not the patients. In 1980, doctors in Germany worked out a new treatment that didn't involve anything going inside the patient – they used a special kind of sound wave that made the stones break up into tiny pieces. Good news for patients, bad news for nutcracker factories.

THE FUTURE

My robot butler has just finished laying the table (unfortunately, he tucked it up in bed under a duvet) so is now ready to give you some more predictions.

PREDICTION 1 – YOUR TOILET WILL BE INTELLIGENT.

It won't read you Dickens while you're pooing – but your toilet will be constantly monitoring your wee to keep an eye on the health of your kidneys. It might tell you to drink a bit more water if you're dehydrated, or it might notice that you have an infection or diabetes or something else that means you need to see your doctor. Or it might say, 'Stop weeing on me! I've got feelings, you know?!'

PREDICTION 2 – YOUR GREAT AUNT PRUNELLA WILL FIND OUT THAT YOU BROKE HER VASE.

Eek – I hope not.

> You did WHAT to my vase? I wondered where that had gone! Get me a new one IMMEDIATELY, you hideous specimen. Prunella

ADAM'S ANSWERS

WHICH NURSERY RHYME WAS ALL ABOUT A KIDNEY DOCTOR?

No, it's not 'I'm a Little Wee-pot'. No one's quite certain if this is true (because it was from hundreds of years ago), but historians think that 'Frère Jacques' was named after a bloke called Frère Jacques Beaulieu who wandered around France, cutting out people's kidney stones and unfortunately killing quite a lot of them in the process. The history books don't mention whether he whistled the tune while he cut his patients open.

HOW CAN YOU SAVE A LIFE USING A WASHING MACHINE, SOME CANS OF BEANS AND A FEW OLD SAUSAGES?

By turning them into a dialysis machine, which is basically an artificial kidney that filters people's blood if their kidneys aren't working too well. These days they're a lot more advanced, but the very first dialysis machine was built during the Second World War, when it was extremely difficult to get equipment because all the factories were making things for the war. A doctor called Willem Kolff made it from a washing machine, a few empty cans and some sausage skin (to use as a filter) and suddenly a load of people's lives were saved! Hopefully they didn't smell too much of sausages afterwards.

WHAT WAS UROMANCY?

It's impossible to predict the future unless you've got a robot butler with a future module. But that hasn't stopped greedy people pretending that they can, to earn money. Over the years, some people have done this by reading tea leaves in the bottom of your cuppa, some by studying the palms of your hands, and some by using uromancy, which is . . . looking at your wee. They would check out the pattern of bubbles in a pot of pee and say if you were going to fall in love or have success at work. If you're the sort of person who will wee into a pot for a 'psychic' stranger, then I can make one very accurate prediction about you: you're extremely gullible.

TRUE OR POO?

THREE HUNDRED YEARS AGO, DOCTORS TRIED TO FIX THE BRAIN USING EXTRACTS OF WEE.

POO It wasn't three hundred years ago – it's happening right now. There's a special type of cell called a stem cell, which scientists can turn into any kind of cell in the body, for example brain cells, if the brain has been damaged. You can find these in blood, but it's much easier (and less sore) to get a sample of urine, which also contains stem cells. A few weeks ago, Pippin weed on my pillow – maybe she was just trying to make me cleverer? Sorry, I mean **EVEN** cleverer.

THERE USED TO BE A TAX ON WEE.

TRUE Urine wasn't just used as an unhygienic mouthwash and a disgusting wound-cleaner – lots of different professions were splashing it around too. Romans softened leather with it, used it to make wool and even washed their togas in it (yuck). It was used so much that the emperor eventually decided to make some money out of it – so he put a tax on wee. (Tax is something grown-ups always moan about, but it's actually a good thing – because by paying it you give money to the government so we can have important things like schools and hospitals.)

THE SPLEEN IS RESPONSIBLE FOR YOUR SENSE OF HUMOUR.

POO Your brain is responsible for your sense of humour, and your spleen is all about getting rid of damaged red blood cells. Well, we know that now. Even though he made lots of great discoveries, William Harvey thought that giggling was all down to your spleen. It's a shame that isn't true, because if you don't laugh at the jokes in this book I could have claimed it's because your spleen's broken.

CRAZY CURES

Kings have always been obsessed with tricks that would make them stay young, presumably so they could be king forever and ever. King Louis XIV of France, who was known as the Sun King, thought that the secret to eternal youth was having liquids squirted up his bottom. His fave bum liquid was almond milk mixed with honey, and he had this done literally thousands of times, including during meetings. He should probably have been called the Bum King instead of the Sun King.

This chapter was sponsored by the Urine Society. I would like to thank them for providing me with a car shaped like a kidney and a lifetime's supply of toilets.

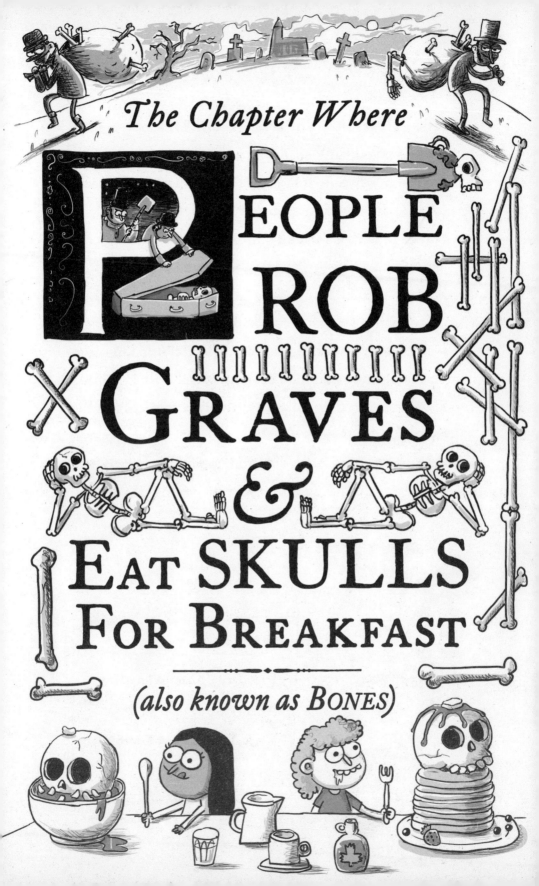

The Chapter Where

PEOPLE ROB GRAVES & EAT SKULLS FOR BREAKFAST

(also known as BONES)

THIS IS PIPPIN'S FAVOURITE CHAPTER of the book – bones! (Well, unless I write a chapter about rolling around in sewage, that is.) If there's one thing we know for sure about our ancestors it's that they definitely had bones. In fact, it's usually all that's left of them. And, for as long as we've had bones, we've been falling off the back of woolly mammoths and breaking them. If you smashed up your arm five thousand years ago, doctors would cover it with clay, which would harden in the sun and keep the bone nice and still until it had mended a few weeks later. Not much has really changed since then, except these days they make plaster casts out of material that's a lot lighter than clay and, more importantly, much easier for your friends to write rude words on.

Do not encourage your readers to write rude words, you vile boy. It's bad enough that you do it, without corrupting all these innocent children. Prunella

NOT OK	OK
BUMHOLE →	ANUS
POO →	FAECES
FART →	FLATULENCE

ANCIENT EGYPT

Normally, when I talk about doctors in Ancient Egypt, it's to tell you how wrong they were about everything and I'll say something like, 'They thought the nose was made of pasta,' or, 'They treated earache by tap-dancing.' But when it came to the bones, they were pretty advanced. They wrote about how to treat a broken collarbone using a sling, exactly the same way we do today. They drew pictures showing a doctor putting a dislocated shoulder (dislocation means a bone has come out of its joint) back into place – another technique that hasn't changed in four thousand years. They even made a prosthetic toe out of wood and leather for someone who'd lost their big toe. (I mean it had been cut off, not that they'd accidentally left it in the supermarket.) It's a bit weird how they got some stuff totally right and the rest completely wrong – maybe an Ancient Egyptian travelled forward in time to medical school, but only went to one lesson and spent the rest of the day in the British Museum, visiting her family.

Unfortunately, the Ancient Egyptians had their limits – if a broken bone burst through the skin or needed screws or pins to fix it, that would almost certainly result in death because, as you know, they didn't have antibiotics or anaesthetics. It makes me extremely glad to be alive today because we have those amazing medical advances and, just as importantly, choc ices. X-rays of King Tutankhamun show that he probably died from a broken leg that wouldn't have been possible for his doctors to fix. (Either that or someone accidentally dropped him down the stairs when he was a mummy.) He was buried with 130 walking sticks to help him in the afterlife – don't you just hate it when you turn up in the afterlife with only 129 walking sticks?

1987

Some archaeologists were exploring a cave in Somerset when they spotted a drinking bowl from about fifteen thousand years ago. Why's this in the bones chapter of this book, not the cutlery and crockery section? Well, firstly, this book doesn't have a cutlery and crockery section. And, secondly, the bowl was made out of a human skull. Luckily, skeleton-based dinnerware has gone out of fashion since then, and these days it's much easier and much less messy to get your bowls from IKEA.

ANCIENT GREECE

In Ancient Greece, they realized the importance of exercise for keeping your body healthy, and your bones and muscles strong. Hippoface was the first doctor ever to write a patient a prescription for exercise. (The patient had TB, so the exercise wasn't particularly helpful and they still died of it, but it's the thought that counts, I guess.) If you've ever seen a picture of a Greek statue, you'll know from their abs that they spent a lot of time working out – they even invented competitions so they could show off how buff they were. You might have heard of a little event called the Olympics? They also came up with the concept of gyms, or to use their proper name, gymnasiums – which means 'place to exercise naked'. (My lawyer, Nigel, has asked me to point out in the strongest terms that you should always wear your gym kit when exercising.)

ANCIENT ROME

The Ancient Romans also thought that exercise was very good for your health, and the three main kinds they recommended were walking, running and . . . reading out loud. Two out of three ain't bad. I'm a big fan of reading, but I'm not sure how it's a form of exercise – unless the book is made from enormous slabs of marble?

Well, reading this book is certainly exhausting. Prunella

Galen did a pretty decent job of figuring out how the muscles worked (I guess they're just underneath the skin, so there's no excuse for messing that one up) and he also sussed out how muscles hang out together in pairs. Before you start thinking he was too much of a genius though – he thought that bones were made from solidified sperm. Umm . . . nope!

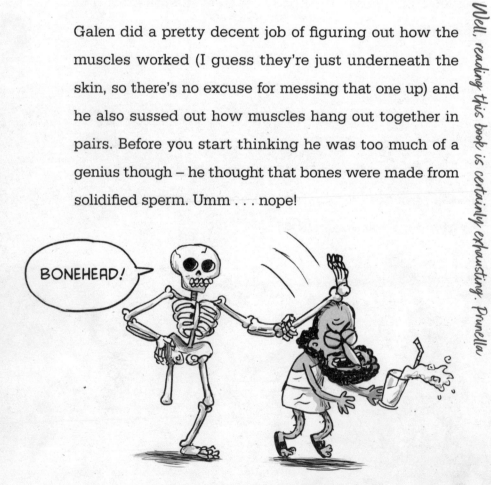

SPARKLE TIME

If you broke a bone in Sparkle Time, they had a much better way of keeping it still than covering it in thick clay, so no one had to walk about with an enormous flower pot on their leg any more. They would soak bandages in horse blood, then wrap them round you. When the blood was all dried up and clotted, the bandages became solid and the leg couldn't move. Clever, right? (But disgusting, obviously.)

You know at Halloween how people eat sweets shaped like skulls and crisps shaped like vampire fangs? Well, back in Sparkle Time, they were into spooky snacks too – there was one popular treat in particular called a mellified man. Sounds quite nice, doesn't it – a bit like a jelly baby? Shall I tell you the recipe?

- Take an extremely old man who's going to die in the next few weeks.
- Ban him from eating or drinking anything apart from loads and loads of honey.
- Make him have a bath of honey every day.

When he dies (probably from eating too much honey), put him in a coffin that's filled to the brim with even more honey.

 Wait one hundred years.

 Cut him up and eat as a delicious, sugary snack.

Would you like some? I'll put you down for a few chunks. Doctors at the time claimed that eating a mellified man could cure broken bones. Personally, I think the only thing it could actually do would be to put you off your dinner for the next thirty years.

CHOP CHOP

Dissection is the word for 'cutting up dead bodies'. This is handy when you're a medical student because if you're out at the shops and one of your friends calls to ask what you're studying at the moment you can say, 'I'm doing dissection,' because 'I'm cutting up dead bodies' might make the other customers freak out and call the police. Dissection is an important part of learning how to be a doctor because bodies are 3D so you can't learn everything about them just from looking at diagrams in books. Well, they could use pop-up books, I suppose.

These days some very kind people say that they're happy for medical students to learn how to be doctors by dissecting their bodies after they die, knowing that this will help thousands of patients in the future. But it wasn't always like this . . .

For a start, in Sparkle Time, it was illegal to dissect anyone. This made it pretty tricky to train up doctors, and even trickier to discover anything new about the body. After hundreds of years of the medical schools stamping their feet and banging on the table and

317

moaning that this rule was **SO UNFAIR**, the government eventually allowed people to be cut up. But they only allowed ten people a year to be dissected in the whole country, which wasn't enough. Imagine if there were only ten laptops to share among every school in the country – you wouldn't learn very much.

A bit more begging and moaning from the medical schools meant that in 1752 the government decided that anyone who'd been executed for murder could be dissected. But medicine was getting more and more popular because everyone realized that being a doctor was the second-coolest thing in the world. (The coolest thing in the world is being called Adam.) As a result, there weren't enough murderers to go round. Soon the medical schools were getting desperate for bodies and offered money to anyone who could provide them with a corpse or ten. I think you might be able to guess why this was a bad idea . . .

Please welcome (or rather please boo extremely loudly) the bodysnatchers. They would hang around graveyards at night, and dig up recently buried bodies – the fresher the better because medical schools weren't interested in ones that had started to go all manky. Thousands of bodies were stolen, and the police didn't really interfere much because in those days stealing a body was an extremely minor crime. The bodysnatchers left the dead person's clothes and jewellery inside the coffin because it was a much bigger crime to steal those than the body itself . . . Weird. Medical schools would pay about £7 for a body in good condition – which might only be enough to buy a pizza now, but back then was tons of money (the equivalent of about £1,000 now, so **LOADS** of pizzas).

Families who were worried about their loved ones getting pilfered would bury them in iron coffins that were much harder to break open, or padlock their bodies into the coffins. Some would even set up a complicated booby-trap system involving tripwires that set off guns. But all this did was make the bodysnatchers more inventive: for example, digging tunnels underground to get to the coffins.

STILL FINDING THIS A BIT CREEPY.

It also meant that they would steal from poorer graves, because their families couldn't afford to protect the people they'd buried.

The most famous bodysnatchers were called William Burke and William Hare, who probably met at the People Called William Society. In 1828, they worked out a short cut for selling bodies to the medical school where they lived in Edinburgh, without having to go down to the graveyard and get their shoes covered in mud. That's right – they'd murder people. In one year, they killed sixteen people – most of them rented a room in William Hare's house. If I was renting a room in someone's house, I'd probably get suspicious if the previous fifteen guests had mysteriously disappeared. (My lawyer, Nigel, has asked me to point out that you should never, ever murder people when they're staying in your spare room.)

Burke and Hare eventually got caught (when they left a dead body in a room someone else was staying in – whoops) and Burke was sentenced to death. Hare was let off, even though he was involved in the murders, because he gave evidence against Burke. The story of the murders was such a scandal that around 25,000 people came to watch Burke being hanged. I guess there weren't any pop concerts to go to in those days. In a bit of a twist, Burke's own body was dissected at the medical school – well, he was a murderer after all. His skeleton has been on display at the Anatomical Museum in Edinburgh ever since!

Is this chapter not finished yet? I've fallen asleep three times reading it. Prunella

CRACK, CRUNCH, OUCH!

In the 1700s, if you'd dislocated a joint or broken a bone that needed to be wiggled back into the right position before you got your plaster cast, then you'd probably go to a bonesetter. They weren't trained as doctors, but on the plus side they were much cheaper.

One of the most famous and popular bonesetters was a lady called Crazy Sally. Would you want to go to get your broken arm fixed by someone with **CrAzY** written on their door? I think I'd prefer to see Sensible Susan.

2013

Doctors have been making artificial limbs for thousands of years, for people who were born without arms or legs, or patients who lost them in accidents or operations. Early artificial limbs were made out of things like iron (a bit heavy) and horses' legs (a bit weird) but technology has come a long way since then. In 2013, a man had an artificial arm fitted that's controlled by signals from his brain – it sounds like science fiction, but it's science fact. The technology for his arm cost nearly £100,000,000, so he'd better not accidentally leave it on the bus.

I CAN SEE RIGHT THROUGH YOU

If you've ever broken a bone, you'll probably remember the very important thing that happened soon afterwards. No, not getting the day off school. No, not getting an extra portion of ice cream. No, not complaining that it was vanilla ice cream when you really wanted triple chocolate fudge supreme. Look – this is the section about X-rays: stop talking about ice creams. I obviously mean you got an X-ray.

But if you broke a bone before 1895, then you wouldn't have had an X-ray – because they hadn't been discovered yet. Actually, if you broke a bone before 1895, then you're over 130 years old and you're outside the recommended reading age range for this book – please give it to someone younger **IMMEDIATELY**. X-rays were invented by Wilhelm Röntgen. It took me nearly forty minutes to work out how to do the letter ö on my computer. I might do a few more so it wasn't a total waste of my time: ÖÖÖÖÖÖÖÖÖÖÖÖÖÖÖÖÖÖÖÖÖÖÖ.

NÖÖÖÖÖÖÖÖÖ!

WILHELM RÖNTGEN: FIVE FACTS AND A LIE

1. He got kicked out of school for drawing a rude cartoon of a teacher. This was very unfair because one of his friends had actually drawn it. It's a bit like when I got in trouble for pouring jam into the toaster when it was actually my brother who did it. I'm still cross about that, to be honest.

2. Things that have been named after him include a mountain in the Antarctic, a chemical element and a range of delicious chocolate bars.

3. He refused to make any money from X-rays because he wanted the whole world to benefit. What a nice bloke.

4. He won the first-ever Nobel Prize for his discovery. I've not won any Nobel Prizes, which is very mean because there's a Nobel Prize for literature and I've written the best books in the world. —

→ *Ahem. Prunella*

5. He spent seven weeks working uninterrupted in total silence before he made his big discovery, stopping only to eat meals and for the occasional nap. (I'm **ALMOST** the same – when I write books, I only stop every ten minutes to eat a snack or watch TV.)

6. The first X-ray ever taken was of his wife's hand. She screamed, 'I have seen my death!' which is fair enough because she was the first person who'd ever looked at their own skeleton. (Apart from people who've had some kind of terrible injury.)

2. He got the mountain (Röntgen Peak) and the element (roentgenium), but sadly no range of chocolate bars. He must be absolutely gutted.

HIP HIP HOORAY

X-rays meant that doctors finally knew what was going on inside their patients' smashed-up legs, and they could come up with better plans than 'chuck a plaster cast on it and hope for the best'. It meant they could rummage around in their toolbox for things to use, like nails and screws, and – thanks to newly discovered anaesthetics and antibiotics – their patients even stood a chance of living long enough to walk around on their newly fixed legs.

Not everything can be fixed so easily though. For example, I once accidentally smashed my Great Aunt Prunella's precious vase when I was practising tennis in her living room. Sometimes joints are damaged so badly that they need to be replaced. The first successful hip replacement was performed in 1938 by a surgeon called Philip Wiles, who made a new hip joint from steel. These days, most hip replacements are performed because when people get old their joints can wear out a bit and become painful. Over half a million hips are replaced every single year, and that's not to mention the artificial knees and shoulders and ankles and elbows and wrists and bums. Not bums, actually – I meant to say thumbs.

So that's how it broke! How many times have I told you not to play tennis inside?! Prunella

1923

You know how I mentioned the first *successful* hip replacement? That kind of suggests there might have been some less successful attempts . . . such as Marius Smith-Petersen who made a new hip joint out of glass in 1923. Unsurprisingly, this didn't work, and his poor patient's hip smashed into smithereens. Honestly, what was he thinking? He might as well have made it out of chocolate.

THE FUTURE

It's prediction time, so let's hear what my robot butler has to say. He's just been lacing my shoes (unfortunately, he's decorated them all over with lace).

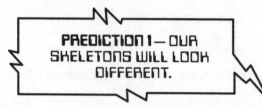

PREDICTION 1 – OUR SKELETONS WILL LOOK DIFFERENT.

If you're anything like me, you'll look in the mirror and think it's impossible for humans to be any more perfect. But humans have been evolving for millions of years, since we looked like monkeys and ate triceratops for tea, and we're showing no sign of stopping now.
For example, the less we exercise, the smaller our bones will get. Scientists have already noticed that our elbows are shrinking slightly. Quick, do some more elbow exercises! And the amount of time we spend bent forward, looking at screens, is changing the shape of our skulls: we're developing an enlarged occipital protuberance. (Or, in English, the bump on the back of our heads is getting bigger.) To be honest, I was hoping for a slightly more exciting evolution than thinner

elbows and a bumpier head – being able to fly, maybe?
Making teachers disappear by clicking our fingers? A
nose that produces candyfloss instead of snot?

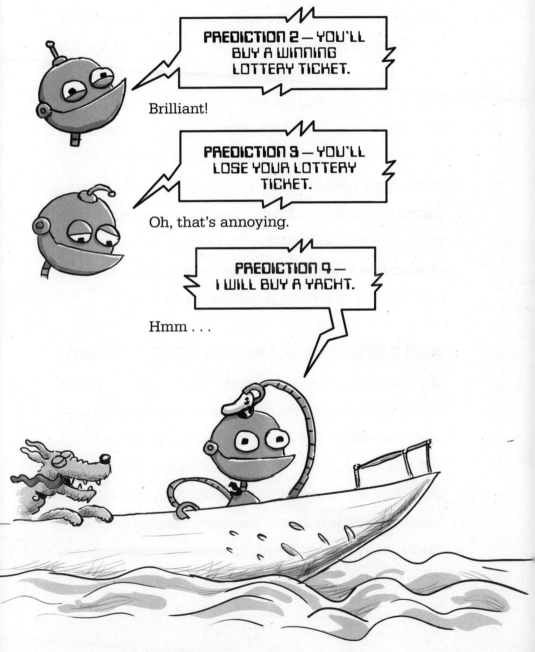

PREDICTION 2 – YOU'LL
BUY A WINNING
LOTTERY TICKET.

Brilliant!

PREDICTION 3 – YOU'LL
LOSE YOUR LOTTERY
TICKET.

Oh, that's annoying.

PREDICTION 4 –
I WILL BUY A YACHT.

Hmm . . .

ADAM'S ANSWERS

WHY ARE WE TALLER THAN OUR ANCESTORS?

I don't know if you've ever been to a museum where they've got a really, really, really old bedroom on display, but you might have noticed that the beds were absolutely tiny. I remember seeing one that was only the size of a matchbox. No, hang on, that might have been a doll's house. Anyway, what I'm trying to say is that we're a lot bigger than we used to be. The reason is that in the olden days people's growth was affected by having serious illnesses in childhood and not getting enough food or vitamins. Today we're on average nine centimetres taller than people were a hundred years ago. And we've got much better clothes now too.

WHAT CAN WE FIND OUT BY LOOKING AT OLD BONES?

Quite a lot! Bones are almost as revealing as your great aunt's secret diary, which you definitely shouldn't have read, that tells you she kissed a soldier the night before she married Great Uncle Malcolm. Even if bones are hundreds of thousands of years old, they can tell us if they belonged to a man or a woman, how old they were, the various illnesses they had, how they died and their favourite song. (OK, fine, I made the last one up.) And

→ *Delete this! You horrible, miserable little shrimp. Prunella*

finally, if you find a load of bones in a suitcase underneath the floorboards in your living room, then that means you live with a murderer and should probably call the police.

WHO HAS THE WORLD RECORD FOR BREAKING THE MOST BONES?

I mean the person who broke the most of their own bones, by the way, not some hammer-wielding maniac. A man called Evel Knievel managed to break 433 bones while doing his job. That's quite a lot when you consider that the body only has 206 bones. What was the job that resulted in so many broken bones? He worked in a supermarket and a big pile of baked-bean cans fell on him every single shift. I made that up, actually: he was a stunt motorcyclist, who would drive off ramps and fly over long lines of cars. And obviously crash quite often.

OOH, THAT'S HANDY!

HOSPITAL

TRUE OR POO?

KING CHARLES II WAS A CANNIBAL.

TRUE He didn't munch on people's arms like lamb chops or eat people's eyeballs as if they were grapes, but Charlie boy was a fan of something called 'the King's Drops'. If he was feeling a bit groggy when he woke up, he'd pop some of this lovely liquid on his tongue: alcohol mixed with crushed-up bits of human skull. Maybe it's just me, but if I'm feeling rubbish in the morning I have a big glass of water and a bit of a lie-in.

DOCTORS USED TO INJECT JOINTS WITH GOLD.

TRUE There's a condition called rheumatoid arthritis that makes some people's joints swell up and become really painful. About eighty years ago, the best treatment was to inject affected joints with gold. These days there are much more effective medicines available, so there's no need to melt down your great aunt's earrings and stab them into your knee, which I'm sure you'll be pleased to hear. —— *Don't you dare! Prunella*

THE ANCIENT ROMANS KNEW THAT THE BONES MADE BLOOD CELLS.

POO You obviously know that the body's blood cells are made in the bone marrow in the middle of our bones. (If you didn't know, you can just pretend that you did – I'll never find out.) Back in Ancient Rome, they had no idea about this – they actually thought the bone marrow was full of old, used-up, useless bits of bone, and they called it *excrementum ossium*. Hold on. I'm just going to look up *excrementum ossium* in a Latin dictionary to find out what it means . . . OMG. It means 'bone-poo'!

CRAZY CURES

If you had sore, swollen joints – known as arthritis – hundreds of years ago, the treatment used to be to smear fat all over them. Chicken fat, maybe? Elephant fat? Nope – human fat, delivered fresh by the nearest executioner. That's really quite revolting, and it obviously didn't work, but doctors back then could have actually been on to something – scientists have recently discovered that injecting some smooshed-up fat directly into joints might help people with arthritis.

The Chapter With

GOAT'S WEE,

MAGIC LASERS

& A LITTLE DROP OF

PIGEON BLOOD

(also known as EYES AND EARS)

I PRESUME I DON'T NEED TO EXPLAIN what your eyes are? Big circles at the front of your face that you see out of? Well, humans have been trying to work out how they work ever since our great-great-great-great-great-great-great . . . actually, can you just imagine a load of 'greats' there, otherwise I'll run out of pages in this book? Ever since our hundreds-of-greats-grandparents were around.

ANCIENT EGYPT

The Ancient Egyptians didn't have a clue how the eyes actually worked, but they knew that lots of things could go wrong with them.

What do you first think of when I say 'Ancient Egypt'? OK, fine, pharaohs. Well, how about the second thing? Mummies, eh? How about the third thing, then? Pyramids? Oh, forget it. I meant sand. It was very common for people back then to have sight loss, partly because of the wind whipping all that sand into their eyes (ouch) and also because of infections that they didn't have any treatments for. That's what all their heavy make-up was about – they weren't going trick-or-treating every day of the week. They thought it contained chemicals that would prevent infections, and would keep dust out of their eyes.

If someone did lose their sight, the doctors had a couple of tricks up their sleeves. The first one was to mash up some tortoise brain, combine it with honey and spread it on the poorly eye. The second option was to kill a pig, pull out its eye and say a spell which would magically transfer the pig's vision into the patient's eye. I don't know exactly how the spell went, but it was probably something like:

> This will make your eyes work,
> Unless I am mistaken.
> Then after let's have dinner:
> There's tortoise or there's bacon.

But unfortunately for the patients (and the pigs and the tortoises) none of this made the slightest bit of difference to anyone's sight.

We know that back in Ancient Egypt there were many successful blind musicians and poets – just like today, sight loss didn't have to stop people doing what they wanted.

ANCIENT INDIA

Remember Sushruta from back in the surgery chapter? Well, he was also a bit of an eye boffin, and invented an operation to help people with cataracts. Cataracts aren't cats who do acrobatics – cataracts are a condition that people sometimes get when they're older, where the lens of the eye goes white, instead of see-through. And if the lens isn't see-through, then you can't see through it . . . Sushruta's method of removing cataracts meant his patients could see again, and it wasn't too different from the way that surgeons remove them today. Not bad for two thousand years ago!

ANCIENT ROME

Galen thought he'd totally worked out what made people go blind. Here's the list:

1. Drawing.
2. Writing for too long.
3. Smelly farts.

I'm pretty sure he got this wrong because I've been sitting writing this book for weeks with Pippin farting away constantly by my feet, and my eyesight seems totally fine.

On the plus side, by then they'd cut up enough eyeballs to work out all the different parts of the eye, although they reckoned the lens was the bit that detected light, rather than the . . . Go on – what part of the eye detects light?

The retina. You knew that, right? Sure, I believe you.

NOT EYEDEAL

Not everyone can be great at their job. In fact, some people are absolutely terrible. For example, before I was a doctor, I worked in a newsagent's at weekends, and one day I fell asleep at the till and someone came in and stole a load of Twixes. (My lawyer, Nigel, has asked me to point out that stealing Twixes – and indeed any form of chocolatey delight – is a very serious crime.)

These days doctors have to do loads and loads of annoying exams to make sure they're good enough, but in the olden days the rules weren't so strict, so there were some absolute losers working in medicine. One of the very worst was a man called John Taylor, who was an eye surgeon in the 1700s. He didn't think the name John Taylor sounded cool enough, so he called himself 'Chevalier' instead and travelled around Europe in a coach decorated with loads of eyes. (Bit weird, John.)

Anyway, he might have been better off calling himself 'Eye Destroyer' because he was a really, really, **REALLY** terrible surgeon. He blinded hundreds of the patients he operated on, thanks to his bad surgery and his insistence on giving everyone eyedrops made from pigeon blood.

1972

A university in Germany
was doing eye tests on its students
when they noticed that a pupil called
Veronica Seider had incredible vision.
She could read writing that was so tiny that
anyone else would need a microscope to see
it, and she could describe the faces of people
who were standing over a mile away. No one
had a clue how she was able to see so well
(maybe she ate a lorry full of carrots every
evening?) but she's in the *Guinness
Book of Records* for having the best
eyesight in history.

This didn't stop him, and he somehow attracted lots of celebrity clients, including the world's most famous composers. He operated on J. S. Bach (who wrote pieces including *Toccata and Fugue in D minor*, *The Well-tempered Clavier*, and *Pippin is the Smelliest Dog in the World*). Unfortunately, the surgery blinded him (eek) and killed him (double eek). Another composer he took his knife to was Handel (who wrote the *Messiah*, *Water Music* and *I Can't Understand Why She's So Smelly – Is It Something We're Feeding Her?*) and unfortunately totally blinded him too.

ALL HAIL BRAILLE

In 1824, Louis Braille developed a system that helped people who are blind or have limited vision to read. He called it Braille (why did everyone name their inventions after themselves?) and to read it you run your fingers over little bumps on the page, which spell out the words. He got the idea from 'night writing' that some soldiers in the French army used so they could pass notes to each other in the dark – proper important soldiery notes, not things people pass around in class like 'You smell', which in Braille would be ⠽⠕⠥ ⠎⠍⠑⠇⠇

Louis Braille's original system is still used today, pretty much unchanged. Next time you're with an adult at a cash machine, have a look at the keypad and you'll see the numbers are also written in Braille.

LOUIS BRAILLE: FIVE FACTS AND A LIE

1. Louis lost his sight when he was three by playing with sharp tools in his dad's workshop. (That's why you should never mess around with sharp objects!)
2. He went to the world's first-ever school for blind people, called the Institut National des Jeunes

Aveugles (or the National Institute for Blind Children, if you're not as amazing at French as I am).

3. He invented Braille when he was only fifteen. When I was fifteen, I did my grade three piano, which is almost as impressive.

4. Louis Braille's face was on a special dollar coin, which also had the word Braille written on it in Braille.

5. He was a brilliant musician who played the organ in churches all over France, and developed a special type of Braille for reading music.

> *That sentence has the word Braille in it too many times. Prunella*

6. He wrote the first pages of Braille by using an owl's beak.

6. *No owls were harmed during the development of Braille. His first pages of Braille were written using an awl, which is actually the same woodworking tool that caused him to lose his sight when he was younger.*

SPECS EDUCATION

The first spectacles were made in Italy some time around 1300 – the year, I mean, not one o'clock in the afternoon. Before then, I guess everything just looked a bit blurry. No one knows exactly who invented them, so maybe I should just pretend that I did. (Yes, I **do** look great for 750 years old, don't I?) You had to hold these early glasses up to your face if you wanted to use them, or balance them on your nose, which wasn't very convenient, but better than nothing, I guess. Later versions included the pince-nez (which means 'pinch-nose' – I told you I was amazing at French) that clamped onto your nose like a peg so they didn't fall off, but made you sound as if you had a terrible cold all the time. Then there's the monocle, which you just balance in one eye socket. They're a bit weird and not very popular these days: my Great Aunt Prunella is the only person I've ever seen who wears one.

In the 1700s, opticians finally remembered that people have ears, and started making glasses with arms on like we have today.

> How dare you make fun of my beautiful monocle in front of all these readers. Prunella

EARLY GLASSES

PINCE-NEZ

MONOCLE

PINEAPPLE THEMED

VIRTUAL REALITY

We used to think that contact lenses were invented in the 1940s, but then somebody was having a rummage in Leonardo da Vinci's old notebooks and spotted that he'd invented them over four hundred years earlier. We should probably have a careful look through everything he wrote, just in case he also invented the infinite ice-cream machine or flying trousers.

1988

The first-ever laser eye surgery was carried out on a patient in New York. It worked by making tiny adjustments to the cornea at the very front of the eye. It's extremely effective at improving people's eyesight . . . but would **you** want to be the first-ever patient to have a laser blasted into your eyes?

EARS

Unlike the brain or the heart or almost any other body part really, humans have always known what their ears were for. Throughout history, if someone's parents were telling them to clean up their cave or pyramid or whatever, then sticking their fingers in their ears meant they couldn't hear them. Simple.

That doesn't mean they knew how the ears actually worked, or what to do if they weren't hearing so well though. In Ancient Egypt, if someone had difficulty hearing, they'd make up a mixture of olive oil, ants' eggs, goat's wee and bat wings and glug it down their earholes. The weird thing is, that might have actually worked – nothing to do with the ants or the goats or the bats though. Olive oil can help to unclog any earwax that might be causing problems and we still use it today. (I'm so glad that it's olive oil we still use and not goat's wee.)

Hearing aids may be very high-tech now, and so small that you can't even see them, but early versions back in the 1600s were a bit more obvious. They were called ear trumpets, but, instead of blowing into one like a normal trumpet that makes a noise like a rhinoceros farting, people would place the smaller end in their ear and point the wide end at whoever was speaking.

TRUMPET: INVENTED 1500 BC

EAR TRUMPET: INVENTED 1639

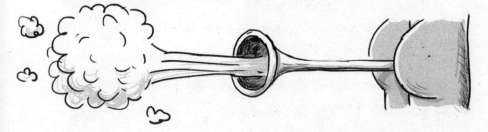

BUM TRUMPET ('BUMPET'): INVENTED 2021

Sign language has been around for about a thousand years, but the first people who used it didn't have hearing difficulties – they were monks who kept a vow of silence in their monasteries. Monk-y sign language

(I'm not sure what it was actually called, but they were monks so I'll call it monk-y sign language) was quite limited because it was mostly phrases they used a lot in their day-to-day monking. For example: 'prayer' and 'bell-ringing' and 'why do we shave big bald patches on the tops of our heads?' In the 1500s, some Native American communities developed a complete sign language, but it took Britain a couple of hundred years to catch on – typical. Today over 150,000 people in the UK communicate using British Sign Language – why don't you learn a few words? (No, not bum. No, not that word either. Or that word.)

1977

An engineer at NASA called Adam Kissiah had hearing loss, but unfortunately his doctors didn't know any treatments that would work for him. So he thought, *I'm a NASA engineer – I can sort this out myself*, and spent every lunchtime coming up with a solution. What he invented was called a cochlear implant – a special type of hearing aid that transmits sound waves deep into the inner ear and now helps tens of thousands of people to hear. See, all the main geniuses are called Adam. ⟶

That's untrue. In my experience, it's a name associated with total numbskulls. Prunella

THE FUTURE

My robot butler has just been running a bath (unfortunately, he put it on a treadmill and smashed it).

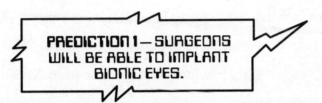

PREDICTION 1 — SURGEONS WILL BE ABLE TO IMPLANT BIONIC EYES.

Scientists are already working on bionic eyes that can send pictures directly to patients' brains. These don't just have the potential to restore sight to people who have lost theirs, but could even give them super-vision that would allow them to zoom in on huge distances, see at night and show heat patterns. (Which means you'll be able to tell if someone has farted.)

PREDICTION 2 — YOU'RE GOING TO FORGET TO WATER THE PLANT ON YOUR DESK.

Good point.
I'll water it now.
Or maybe later.

WATER ME!   DON'T FORGET!

ADAM'S ANSWERS

WHY WOULD AN EYE DOCTOR GIVE YOU DEADLY POISON?

Because they're evil and want to kill you. Or, alternatively, they might just want to dilate your pupils (make them go bigger) so they can have a better look inside your eyes. Doctors have known for thousands of years about a plant that can kill you if you eat it, but will make your pupils dilate if you put it in your peepers. There are lots of names for this plant, including deadly nightshade, devil's berries and death cherries, but its proper name is belladonna, which means 'pretty woman' (because people used to think that pupils the size of snooker balls were especially beautiful).

WHAT HAPPENED IF YOU WERE A KING WHO WAS HARD OF HEARING?

Well, if it was 1820 and you were King John VI of Portugal and Brazil (a bit greedy being king of two places), then you'd sit on a massive throne that was also a hearing aid. If you wanted to speak to King John, you'd kneel down at his feet and talk into the arms of the chair, which were shaped like lions' mouths. The sound would travel up through the mouths and into little speakers by his ears. He would then reply something like, 'Off with his head!' or, 'Bring me a massive chocolate cake – I'm the king!' Luckily, these days hearing aids are a lot more portable.

TRUE OR POO?

AN AMERICAN PRESIDENT INVENTED A NEW TYPE OF GLASSES.

TRUE Benjamin Franklin (who was president from 1785–1788) needed two different pairs of specs: one for reading things close up and one for looking at stuff that was further away, so he invented a new type of glasses with different lenses in the top and bottom halves. Bingo! He never needed to switch pairs ever again. These glasses are called bifocals and people still wear them today. There's actually a very long tradition of American presidents inventing things. James Madison invented a walking stick with a microscope inside it, so you could inspect any insects that might be scuttling around your feet; George Washington made a machine that planted seeds in fields; Thomas Jefferson built a pasta-making device; and Donald Trump invented a very strange type of hairstyle.

IN ANCIENT GREECE, THEY THOUGHT TEARS WERE CAUSED BY THE BRAIN LEAKING.

POO They actually thought crying meant the heart had been damaged and was turning to water, which somehow whizzed up to the eyes and poured down the face. It took until the 1600s for doctors to discover the tear glands, which probably made a bit more sense, to be honest.

BEETHOVEN COMPOSED MUSIC WHEN HE WAS TOTALLY DEAF.

TRUE Unlike a lot of composers, Beethoven managed to escape being blinded by the operations of John Taylor, but he gradually lost his hearing over a number of years. It started in 1798 when he couldn't hear higher sounds, so the music he wrote became much lower as he got older. When his hearing became even worse, he had to bang the notes on the piano really loudly so he could hear what he was playing, and he accidentally smashed up a lot of pianos (and probably really annoyed his neighbours). Eventually, he became completely deaf, but he was still able to compose music because he could imagine in his head exactly how the tunes would sound.

CRAZY CURES

If you had cataracts in your eyes back in the seventeenth century, you'd have to cross your fingers that you didn't go to see Robert Boyle. He didn't do surgery, or even use eyedrops – his cure was to grind up human poo until it was a brown powder, then blow it into people's eyes. I don't know if he used his own poo or someone else's, but either way it's pretty disgusting.

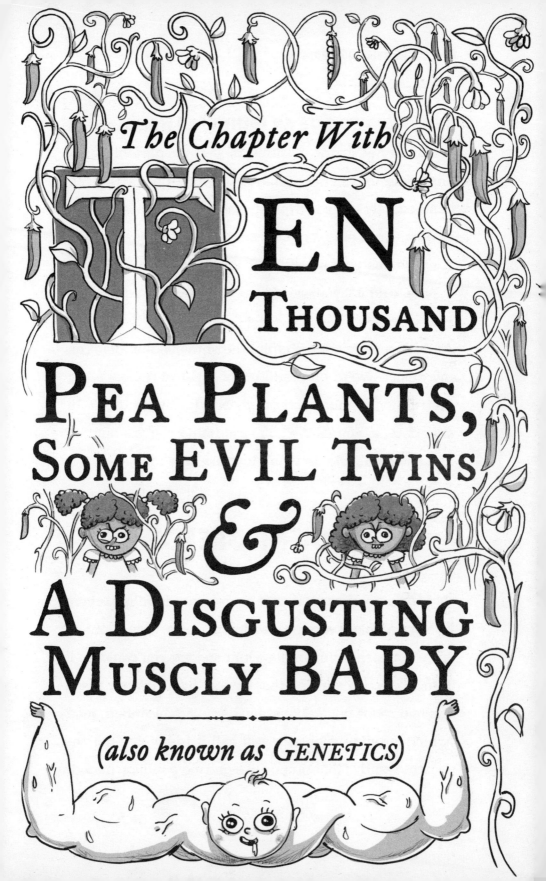

The Chapter With

TEN THOUSAND PEA PLANTS, SOME EVIL TWINS & A DISGUSTING MUSCLY BABY

(also known as GENETICS)

UNLESS YOU'VE GOT AN IDENTICAL TWIN, or an evil scientist has made a clone of you as part of some dastardly experiment, there's nobody on Earth who looks exactly like you. No one else has your nose, no one else has your ears, no one else has your knees, and no one else has your smell. Well, apart from some skunks, maybe. And it's your genes that make you unique.

Thank goodness for that — the last thing we need is loads of people like you running around. Prunella

And not just you. Me, Pippin, the shrivelled-up plant on my desk – we're all made up of a set of genes: a big instruction manual on how to build a living thing. In your case, a human. Well, I'm assuming you're a human. You could be a skunk who's learned how to read.

ANCIENT GREECE

Old Hippoface spotted that there were families where everyone looked very similar: for instance, they might all have a massive chin or nose hair so long you could tie it into a bow. He realized that things like this are passed down through generations, and he called this inheritance, which is what scientists still call it today. It's not the exciting kind of inheritance like getting a million pounds from a long-lost uncle in Venezuela. I wish I had one of those relatives – all Great Aunt Prunella says she'll give me is a horrible lamp with a flamingo on it.

You are the rudest and most ungrateful person I've ever met in my entire life. Now you're not even getting the lamp. Prunella

Hippocrates still got some stuff wrong though – he thought that anything that happened to an adult's body would get passed on to their children – so, if you did loads of weightlifting and ended up with really, really strong arms, then you'd have some kind of disgusting muscly baby.

A BOFFIN WITH A BEARD ON A BOAT

The first person to really shake things up in the genes department was Charles Darwin: back in 1831, he went on a five-year trip round the world on a boat called the HMS *Beagle*, which is a type of dog. I mean a beagle is a type of dog – Charles wasn't sailing around in a massive dog.

His job was to make notes about every rock and plant and animal he saw in all the different places they visited, like a kind of human video recorder. Most of the time though he just sat in his cabin as the boat sailed from place to place – and, because he didn't have any computer games to play or music to listen to, he did a lot of thinking. If I'm left on my own, I normally think things like, *I wonder how many Maltesers you could fit into a car?* or *Who does bigger poos – horses or giraffes?* but Charles started wondering about where we all came from.

HUMAN

HORSE

GIRAFFE

No, not if we're born in Swindon or Sweden or Switzerland, but where we all came from millions of years ago. He cooked up a theory called evolution, which means that we are all descended from the same ancestor. And not just humans! Whether you're the queen or a potato, your maths teacher or a cactus, we all started out the same.

This was quite big news for people one hundred and fifty years ago – no one wanted to be told that their great-great-grandma had a tail and swung from trees – and it caused huge debates. (Debates are what scientists call it when they have massive arguments.)

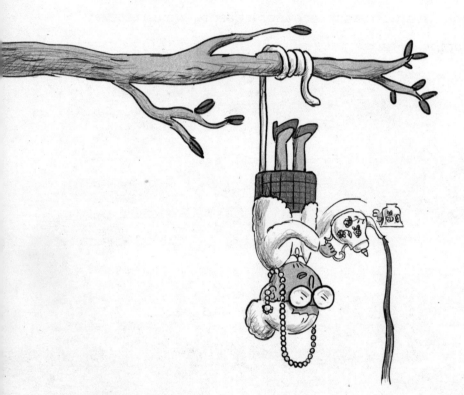

We now know that Charlie was right – and there's lots of proof: it's quite difficult to argue with evolution when you dig up ancient skeletons that are halfway between humans and apes. His theories also explain why certain animals have gone extinct. (RIP dodo, gone too soon, love you babez.)

I NEED A PEA

The next big development in genetics was all thanks to ten thousand pea plants, which showed us exactly how we inherit different characteristics from our parents. Actually, I guess some of the credit should go to a monk called Gregor Mendel who did the experiments on these plants back in the 1850s and 1860s.

Greg's experiments demonstrated for the first time that Hippoface was wrong – it's not all about the dads: you get half your genes from your biological mother and half from Sainsbury's. No, that's not right. I mean you get half your genes from your biological mother and half from your biological father. Greggy also explained why not everything gets passed down through the generations – which is great news for me because my Great Aunt Prunella's nose is so pointy that it smashes windows.

→ *How dare you! I'm writing to your mother about this. Prunella*

When Gregster had finished his experiments, he excitedly published them in 1865, then presumably wondered what to do with all those pea plants, so had a massive dinner of roast peas served with mushy peas with pea gravy and pea crumble for dessert (with pea custard).

Annoyingly, no one believed anything he'd written, so totally ignored it until some other scientists in 1900 realized he was right all along. Unfortunately, by that point he'd been dead for sixteen years. Just as well because he'd have been extremely pea'd off.

D-N-YAY

The next big discovery was DNA, which is short for deoxyribonucleic acid, but we all just say DNA because no one should have to type deoxy*blahblahblah* acid more than once in their lives. DNA is the part of your cells that contains all your genes, wound into a spiral shape, like some kind of cool scientific pasta.

1996

Scientists cloned a sheep for the first time, which means they basically copied and pasted a sheep's DNA to make a brand-new identical one. All sheep look pretty similar to me, so I guess we just have to believe that's what they did. This sheep was called Dolly, which is quite a nice name, but not as good as Adam. Even though she was extremely special, she lived a fairly ordinary life – eating grass, baaing and pooing, like sheep generally do. After she died, she was stuffed and put on display at the National Museum of Scotland in Edinburgh. If you're ever passing by, pop in to see her, although I will warn you that her conversation isn't up to much.

DNA's twisty, twirly shape was discovered by four scientists called Rosalind Franklin, Maurice Wilkins, James Watson and Francis Crick – who all got a Nobel Prize in 1962 apart from Rosalind Franklin, which was very unfair. (She had recently died, and the stupid rules meant she couldn't be recognized for her work.) Understanding DNA's shape meant that scientists could figure out exactly how it worked, how it sometimes goes wrong and, more importantly, how to treat patients whose DNA has gone wonky and caused medical problems.

CANCER

Cancer happens when the genes in a cell have gone wrong and that cell has divided and divided and divided, out of control. Cancer has affected people for a lot longer than we've known about genes – there is evidence of bone cancer in Ancient Egyptian mummies and they wrote about breast cancer on their papyrus scrolls. Sadly, back then cancer was impossible to survive – doctors didn't know what caused it, so they didn't stand a chance of treating it. The invention of anaesthetics and antibiotics meant that surgery was suddenly possible for cancer, but the biggest step forward in treating cancer was the discovery of radiotherapy and chemotherapy.

Radiotherapy is a type of treatment that involves using radioactive substances. You might have already heard about radioactivity at school. Not sure what it is? Well, school is this building that you go into every day during the week where a bunch of boring grown-ups teach you about . . . Oh, you mean radioactivity? Well, that's a special kind of energy given off by certain substances, and it was discovered over a hundred years ago by a Polish scientist who lived in France called Marie Curie.

MARIE CURIE: FIVE FACTS AND A LIE

1. Her university couldn't find her a lab to work in, so she did all her experiments in a leaky, abandoned shed that was previously used for storing dead bodies.

2. She is the only Nobel Prize winner whose daughter has also won a Nobel Prize. No wonder I haven't won a Nobel Prize yet when they keep going to members of the same family.

3. She did a lot of her research with her husband, Barry Curie.

4. She invented the first-ever mobile X-ray machines, which could be used to help soldiers injured in the First World War. Her machines helped over a million soldiers.

5. She discovered two chemical elements: radium and polonium, and a third one was named after her – curium. If I ever discover an element, I'm going to call it AdamIsBrilliantium.

6. The notebooks she wrote in are still too radioactive and dangerous to touch more than one hundred years later, and have to be kept in lead boxes.

3. She did work with her husband, but unfortunately for fans of rhyming names they were Marie and Pierre Curie, not Marie and Barry Curie.

2002

A baby called Rhys Evans was born
with a very rare condition called severe
combined immunodeficiency disorder, which, as
you can probably guess from its name, is very serious
indeed. People with this condition have almost no immune
system, which means that any infection could be extremely
serious. It's also known as 'bubble baby disease' because patients
often have to live inside a plastic bubble to make it less likely that
they'll catch any bugs. Scientists discovered that it was caused by a
problem in Rhys's DNA that meant a gene wasn't working properly.
In 2002, Professor Christine Kinnon led a team that replaced this
faulty gene in Rhys, curing him of his condition, and making him
the first patient in the UK to have this kind of treatment.

Radioactive substances have hundreds of uses in
science, from creating energy to working out what age
dinosaur bones are. But, in medicine, one of the most
important uses is to treat cancer. One of Marie Curie's
colleagues kept a sample of radium in his pocket for a
few hours and then noticed afterwards that the skin
underneath it was badly damaged, so Marie did some
experiments and found out that radioactive substances
kill cells. Usually, this isn't great, but if you're trying to

treat cancer then it's a very good thing. Radiotherapy works because normal cells are good at repairing themselves after they've been blasted with radiation, but cancer cells are usually gone forever.

Chemotherapy is the name for medicines that attack cancer, and they actually came from a very surprising place. No, not the moon. The first chemotherapy drug was made from mustard gas, which was a weapon used in the First World War. People who develop cancer today have a higher chance of survival than ever before thanks to huge advances in surgery, chemotherapy and radiotherapy, often used in combination.

THE FUTURE

My robot butler has been testing the smoke alarms (he asked them to recite their seven times table and name the capital of Belgium) so now he's ready to tell us what the future holds.

PREDICTION 1 – HUNDREDS OF ILLNESSES WILL BE CURED BY FIXING PEOPLE'S DNA.

A lot of illnesses are caused by problems inside our DNA. In fact, it's a bit like the DNA has got a spelling mistake in it. At the moment, scientists are just starting to be able to correct simple errors in DNA, but in the future they'll be able to cure loads of illnesses, from blood disorders to cancer.

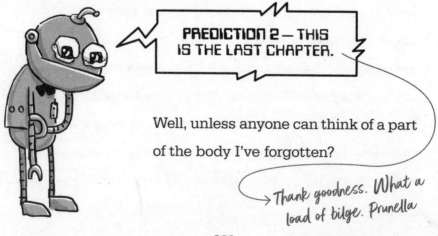

PREDICTION 2 – THIS IS THE LAST CHAPTER.

Well, unless anyone can think of a part of the body I've forgotten?

→ Thank goodness. What a load of bilge. Prunella

ADAM'S ANSWERS

WHERE DOES THE WORD 'CANCER' COME FROM?

It's a word the Ancient Greeks first used that means 'crab'. This is because cancer can spread out with spikes that look a bit like the legs of a crab. Other medical conditions named after animals include lupus (which means 'wolf'), bird flu, chicken pox and Pippin plague.

IS IT POSSIBLE TO CLONE HUMANS?

Yes, it's technically possible – the same technology that worked for Dolly should work for humans too. But it's illegal in most countries, which makes sense, but is a bit of a shame because it would be handy if I had a few clones of me. One could write my books, one could walk Pippin, one could go to the supermarket, and the original me could just go on holiday the whole time.

WHO WORKED OUT WHAT EACH OF OUR GENES DO?

It took a lot of people! Nearly three thousand people worked for thirteen years on something called the Human Genome Project to map out all our genes. They weren't being slow or lazy: they had to look at over three billion bits of DNA, so I guess it's fair enough that it took so many of them.

TRUE OR POO?

JURASSIC PARK COULD ACTUALLY HAPPEN.

POO   Bad news, I'm afraid, if you want a pterodactyl as a pet: DNA has got a best-before date, and if something is as old as a stegosaurus bone then there won't be any DNA left on it whatsoever. It's just as well, I guess – I'm not sure that Pippin would want to share her dinner with a diplodocus.

IT WOULD TAKE YOU A WHOLE MONTH TO TYPE OUT YOUR GENETIC CODE.

POO If you typed at a hundred words per minute (which is really fast), twenty-four hours a day without sleeping or even taking a break to eat a poo or do a sandwich (sorry, wrong way round), then it would take you more than ten years. And you'd be exhausted afterwards. And you'd have missed loads of school. Basically, I don't recommend it.

CHARLES DARWIN WAS AFRAID OF THE SIGHT OF BLOOD.

TRUE Charles Darwin's dad was a doctor and wanted him to go to medical school, so Charles went there so he didn't upset Daddy Darwin. One big problem: Charles was totally terrified of the sight of blood, so he couldn't face going to lessons after a while, and quit his course. It's OK to disagree with your relatives sometimes. For example, my Great Aunt Prunella doesn't think I'm a very good writer, but I still love her very, very much.

Hmm, maybe this book isn't so bad after all — please ignore all my previous comments. I love you too. Prunella

CRAZY CURES

As soon as radium was discovered, people thought it was a magical miracle cure for almost everything. They put it in eyedrops to improve people's vision and even toothpaste to make people's teeth shine bright white. (My lawyer, Nigel, has asked me to point out that you should never use radioactive eyedrops or toothpaste.) It didn't work, obviously. In fact, it made people extremely ill. Even though radioactivity can cure cancer when used correctly, it can actually *cause* cancer if used in random ways like this.

THE BIT

AT THE END

(also known as CONCLUSION)

NOBODY LIKES GOING TO THE DOCTOR'S surgery – let's be honest. Even the doctors don't like it because they have to see a whole load of smelly patients.

But next time you've got a cough or a temperature, or you've hurt your leg, or your bum-spots have got worse, or your head's fallen off, then you should actually thank your lucky stars that you're seeing a doctor **now** and not hundreds of years ago. (This might be tricky if your head has fallen off.)

Because, however cold your doctor's stethoscope or however icky the medicine they give you tastes, at least they won't pluck a chicken's bum and stick it in your armpit or give you some human flesh to eat or make you fart into a jar or put you in a bath full of blood or feed you dog poo or blow smoke up your bum or make you eat millipedes or smear your eye with tortoise brain.

Well, hopefully not. If they do, you have my full permission to run out of the surgery, screaming.

Right – that's the end!

→ *Get out of here. Prunella*

IMPORTANT NOTICE FROM MY LAWYER, NIGEL

Nigel Rosenkrantz

Official lawyer to Dr Adam Kay

One Embassy Gardens

London SW11 7BW

Dr Adam Kay (hereafter referred to as THE GENIUS AUTHOR) strongly advises **you** (hereafter referred to as THE IDIOT READER) against performing actions mentioned in the book, including but not limited to:

1. Sticking a hook up someone's nose to remove their brain.
2. Electrocuting corpses.
3. Drilling holes in skulls.
4. Draining any individual's blood into a bowl.
5. Feeding sponges to a buzzard.
6. Using urine as a mouthwash.
7. Sewing up intestines, using the heads of ants.
8. Eating crushed human bones.

9. Stealing bodies on which to experiment.

10. Cutting up your relatives.

11. Any other action or actions that would be considered illegal.

12. Any other action or actions that would be considered totally disgusting.

Furthermore, THE GENIUS AUTHOR takes no responsibility for any such action or actions performed by THE IDIOT READER. This contract applies in all countries of the world in perpetuity and is legally binding for both humans and dogs.

Signed by THE GENIUS AUTHOR

Signed by THE IDIOT READER

....

Dated ....

ACKNOWLEDGEMENTS

To my husband, James, for only being sick on my laptop once.

To my dog, Pippin, for your incredible support throughout the writing process and beyond.

No, hang on, those two should be the other way round.

To Henry Paker, illustrator to the stars (such as me).

To Cath Summerhayes and Jess Cooper, my awesome agents.

To Ruth Knowles and Emma Jones, my exceptional editors.

To Francesca Dow and Tom Weldon, my phabulous publishers.

To Noah, Zareen, Lenny, Sidney and Jesse – you're getting your names here instead of your birthday presents, soz.

To Hannah Farrell for all her help with factts, and to Justin Myers for saying things like, 'It's actually spelled *facts*.'

And, finally, to YOU! (But only if you think this is the best book you've ever read in your entire life. Otherwise my lawyer, Nigel, insists you have to cross this bit out or face immediate arrest.)

DOCTOROGRAPHY

ADEMOLA, OMO-OBA ADENRELE *(1916–?)* Omo-Oba Adenrele Ademola was born a princess in Nigeria, then trained to be a nurse in London in the 1930s where she worked throughout the Second World War. I really hope she wore her crown on the ward.

AGNODICE *(400 BC)* Back in Ancient Greece, Agnodice was the first-ever female doctor and also the first-ever female midwife. How cool is that? (Very.)

AL-ZAHRAWI, ABU AL-QASIM *(936–1013)* Al-Zahrawi invented loads of the things surgeons use today, such as the scalpel and retractor (which is a kind of surgical instrument, not a type of tractor).

ANDERSON, ELIZABETH GARRETT *(1836–1917)* The first woman to qualify as a doctor in Britain, she also founded the first hospital staffed by women and was the first female mayor. She was really amazing, and more people should know about her – and now **YOU** do!

APGAR, VIRGINIA *(1909–1974)* Inventor of the Apgar Score, a check for newborn babies. When you were born, a doctor or midwife will have checked your Apgar score to see how healthy you were. (I got eight out of ten, fact fans.)

ARISTOTLE *(384–322 BC)* One of the cleverest people of all time, Aristotle worked out loads of human anatomy. His nickname was 'the Mind', which makes him sound like some kind of evil supervillain (but he was good, honestly).

AVICENNA (IBN SINA) *(980–1037)* A well-known Persian and Islamic scientist who wrote *The Canon of Medicine*, one of the most important books ever about cannons. I mean, medicine.

BANTING, FREDERICK *(1891–1941)* and **BEST, CHARLES** *(1899–1978)* Banting and Best won a Nobel Prize in 1923 for making insulin as a treatment for diabetes. Four hundred million people around the world have diabetes, and they all say thank you. (Or *merci*, or *grazie*, or ඔයාට ස්තූතියි.)

BARNARD, CHRISTIAAN *(1922–2001)* Barnard performed the first successful human-to-human heart transplant operation. (He also tried a baboon-to-human heart transplant, but that didn't go so well . . .)

BLUNDELL, JAMES *(1790–1878)* The first doctor to successfully use a blood transfusion to treat a patient for blood loss after childbirth. He had a lie-in until lunchtime every single day, which I'm very jealous about.

BRAILLE, LOUIS *(1809–1852)* Braille developed a system that helped people who are blind or have limited vision to read. Braille is still around today (the language, not the person – he's extremely dead).

COOKE WRIGHT, JANE *(1919–2013)* A scientist who discovered new and better ways to treat cancer, including pioneering ways of using chemotherapy. Her work has saved millions of lives.

CORI, GERTY *(1896–1957)* The first woman to be awarded the Nobel Prize in Medicine. Gerty Cori found out how energy is transported around the body. (Turns out it's not in tiny taxis.)

COUNEY, MARTIN *(1869–1950)* Couney exhibited premature babies in incubators at fairgrounds. A bit weird, but he saved the lives of over six thousand babies, so I'll let him off.

CURIE, MARIE *(1867–1934)* Marie Curie discovered two elements, invented mobile X-ray machines and was one of the most important people in the history of treating cancer. She won two Nobel Prizes for all this, which is fair enough really.

DARWIN, CHARLES *(1809–1882)* He came up with the theory of evolution and explained why some animals survive and some become extinct. One of his favourite meals was armadillos, so it's a miracle that they aren't extinct.

DA VINCI, LEONARDO *(1452–1519)* Da Vinci drew amazing pictures of human anatomy, which helped the world understand the human body much better. He also invented the parachute, the helicopter, solar power, the tank and the calculator. A bit of a show-off, if you ask me.

DERHAM, JAMES *(1762–1802)* James Derham was the first African American doctor. He was born into slavery but went on to have his own successful medical practice and was very important in the fight against racism.

ELION, GERTRUDE *(1918–1999)* Gertrude Elion developed loads of life-saving and life-changing drugs, including treatments for leukaemia and AIDS.

FLEMING, ALEXANDER *(1881–1955)* Discovered the first antibiotic drug, penicillin, when mould grew in his lab. Proof that you should never do the washing-up.

FRANKENSTEIN, VICTOR *(1818–?)* Stitched loads of dead bodies together to make a monster, then brought it to life using lightning. You've got to have a hobby, I guess. (Might have just been a character in a book.)

FRANKLIN, ROSALIND *(1920–1958)*, **WILKINS, MAURICE** *(1916–2004)*, **WATSON, JAMES** *(1928–)* and **CRICK, FRANCIS** *(1916–2004)* Franklin, Wilkins, Watson and Crick discovered the shape of DNA. They called the shape a 'double helix'. I'd have called it a 'wibbly wobbly spiral', but that's probably why I've never won a Nobel Prize.

GALEN *(129–210)* A doctor in Roman times whose ideas and discoveries taught doctors what to do for over a thousand years. (Unfortunately lots of his ideas were wrong. Oops.)

GRAY, HENRY *(1827–1861)* Writer of the medical textbook *Gray's Anatomy*, which is still used today to teach anatomy to doctors. He stole the name of his book from *Kay's Anatomy*, which was a pretty rude thing to do.

HARVEY, WILLIAM *(1578–1657)* One of the first people to work out how blood is pumped around the body. (The answer is 'by the heart'. If you didn't know that, then go and sit in a bin full of worms.)

HIPPOCRATES *(460–375 BC)* Known as the 'Father of Medicine' to thousands of doctors (and known as 'Hippoface' to readers of this book).

HUA TUO *(140–208)* The first doctor to use anaesthetics for surgery in China. He also invented a type of martial arts, so I bet his patients always paid their bills on time.

IBN AL-NAFIS *(1213–1288)* Nearly one thousand years ago in Egypt, Ibn al-Nafis sussed out circulation. Unfortunately no one remembered this, so people got it wrong for centuries afterwards.

JEKYLL, HENRY *(1886–?)* A very well-respected doctor who sometimes drank a special potion and turned into a murderer called Mr Hyde. A bit naughty, to be honest. He was fictional though, so don't have nightmares.

JENNER, EDWARD *(1749–1823)* Invented the first-ever vaccine. Some people were worried that if they took one of his vaccines they'd sprout a cow's head. (They didn't – vaccines are super safe.)

KAY, ADAM *(1980–)* The main doctor you need to know about. Much more important than any of the other losers.

LAENNEC, RENÉ-THÉOPHILE-HYACINTHE *(1781–1826)* Invented the stethoscope. He was probably also the first doctor to say 'Sorry, this is really cold!' when he put it on a patient.

LISTER, JOSEPH *(1827–1912)* Joseph Lister invented the blister. Not really – he did work out that using antiseptic in operations saved lives though.

MENDEL, GREGOR *(1822–1884)* An Austrian monk and botanist who studied inheritance by experimenting with fleas. No, not fleas – peas. Still a bit weird, if you ask me.

METRODORA *(around 200–400 BC)* The first-ever woman to write a medical textbook. Probably known as Dora to her mates.

MOODY, HAROLD *(1882–1947)* Harold Moody was born in Jamaica, then travelled to England to train as a doctor.

He spent his life campaigning against racism and, brilliantly, he changed laws that discriminated against people because of the colour of their skin.

NIGHTINGALE, FLORENCE *(1820–1910)* The founder of modern nursing. She made huge improvements to hospital conditions and saved more lives than I can count. (Then again, I can only count to about fifty.)

PARÉ, AMBROISE *(1510–1590)* A French surgeon who invented tons of operations and was very interested in gunshot wounds. (I mean treating gunshot wounds, not giving people them.)

PASTEUR, LOUIS *(1822–1895)* Louis Pasteur proved that infections come from germs, and invented a way to get rid of them, which made milk safe to drink. So if you like drinking milk, say, 'Thanks, Louis!' Or if you hate drinking milk, say, 'I hate you, Louis!'

PRUNELLA, GREAT AUNT *(1929–)* A moaning old woman who always criticizes my writing.

I'm still reading this, you know?!

RÖNTGEN, WILHELM *(1845–1923)* Wilhelm won a Nobel Prize for discovering X-rays. Very handy to check if you've broken a bone or swallowed a sofa.

SEACOLE, MARY *(1805–1881)* Mary trained as a nurse in Jamaica and saved the lives of hundreds of wounded soldiers in the Crimean War by riding into battle on horseback to treat them. (I don't know the name of her horse, I'm afraid. Cloppy, maybe?)

SEMMELWEIS, IGNAZ *(1818–1865)* Sometimes the simplest things are the most effective. Ignaz told surgeons to wash their hands and – hey presto! – all the patients stopped dying.

SHERLOCK, SHEILA *(1918–2001)* The UK's first female Professor of Medicine. She did loads of research that taught us how the liver works. Not related to Sherlock Holmes.

SORANUS *(100 AD)* An Ancient Greek doctor who wrote textbooks about pregnancy and childbirth. Not to be confused with Uranus, which is a planet.

STRANGE, STEPHEN *(1963–)* The Sorcerer Supreme and primary protector of Earth against magical and mystical threats. Looks quite a lot like Benedict Cumberbatch, if you ask me. Slightly fictional. OK, completely fictional.

SUSHRUTA *(600 BC)* If you suddenly wake up two thousand years ago and need to amputate someone's arm or repair their cataracts, then, luckily for you, Sushruta has written loads of books to teach you how to do it.

TU YOUYOU *(1930–)*, **CAMPBELL, WILLIAM C.** *(1930–)* and **ŌMURA, SATOSHI** *(1935–)* Shared a Nobel Prize for inventing drugs to treat the awful disease malaria, which kills half a million people every year.

WHO, DOCTOR *(1963–)* An extraterrestrial being who explores the universe in a time-travelling spaceship called the TARDIS and hopes that Daleks don't exterminate him. (David Tennant was the best one, and I will not be entering into discussions about this.) Yeah, yeah, he's fictional too.

ZHANG ZHONGJING *(150–219)* One of the most important doctors in Chinese medicine. He also invented dumplings, making him my favourite doctor in all of history (except for me).

INDEX

My favourite pages!

Oi!

Oi again!

> *This is stupid. Stop it now. Prunella*

CREDITS

INVENTORY
Katherine Whelan

PRODUCTION
Naomi Green
Michael Martin
Erica Pascal
Jamie Taylor

FINANCE
Aimee Buchanan
Duc Luong

CONTRACTS
Mary Fox

RIGHTS
Maeve Banham
Bethany Copeland
Susanne Evans
Beth Fennell Alice
Grigg Millie Lovett
Lena Petzke

SALES
Kat Baker
Hannah Best
Toni Budden
Karin Burnik
Ruth Burrow
Autumn Evans
Han Ismail
Lorraine Levis

Geraldine McBride
Sophie Marston
Sarah Roscoe
Rozzie Todd
Becki Wells

MARKETING & COMMUNICATIONS
Simon Armstrong
Roma Baig
Dusty Miller
Jannine Saunders
Tania Vian-Smith

BIBLIOGRAPHIC METADATA
Lauren Floodgate
Jack Lowe

OPERATIONS
Lewis Pearce
Sally Rideout

PRINTERS
David Banks
Bart Chrzanowski
Richard Diaz
Ruby King
Nicola Kingsnorth
Rebecca Lynchsmith
Greg Manterfield-Ivory

ADAM'S LAWYER
Nigel Rosenkrantz

ADAM KAY is a former doctor who has written three million books and sold four copies. No, hang on – he's written four books and sold three million copies.

HENRY PAKER was once a little boy who did silly doodles in the margins of books. Now he is a grown man who does silly doodles in the middle of books.